THAT ALL MAY BE ONE

That All May Be One

Catholic Reflections on Christian Unity

Ernest Falardeau, S.S.S.

PAULIST PRESS
New York/Mahwah, N.J.

Cover design by Nicholas Markell

Library of Congress Cataloging-in-Publication Data

Falardeau, Ernest R.
    That all may be one : Catholic reflections on Catholic unity / Ernest Falardeau.
      p. cm.
    ISBN 0-8091-3925-1 (alk. paper)
    1. Church–Unity–Meditations. 2. Church year meditations–Catholic authors.
I. Title.
BX2170.C55 F25 2000
262'.00'1–dc21
                                               99-056652
                                                 CIP

Published by Paulist Press
997 Macarthur Boulevard
Mahwah, New Jersey 07430

www.paulistpress.com

Printed and bound in the
United States of America

Contents

March: Easter Joy and Christian Unity

April: Pentecost: The Holy Spirit and Unity

May: Mary and Unity

June: The Eucharist: Sign and Means to Unity

July: Marriage and Christian Unity

Contents

Foreword:
An Invitation to Reflect on the
Church through the Year

This volume provides a rich series of very concrete and personal comments on Christ's will for the church, geared to the twelve months of the year. It is for those who preach weekly on the lectionary, who lead new Catholics through the Rites of Christian Initiation for Adults, or who provide religious instruction for adults and young people. These essays will be a rich resource for illustrations, perspectives, and issues to be incorporated in the presentation of the gospel, for the achievement of the church's goal of unity among Christians, and for the enhancement of relationships with the Jewish community.

As Pope John Paul, recalling the Vatican Council, reminds us, conversion to Christ entails conversion to the church and conversion to the church entails zeal for the unity of the churches. The variety of themes in these reflections provide occasions to deepen one's own conversion, and examples to use with others in helping them come to the vision of the church's ecumenical and interfaith commitments today.

The author brings a rich set of experiences to the reader, filling out his understanding of the faith with concrete occasions of repentance, reconciliation and commitment he has experienced in his life with fellow Christians and Jews. The call to full communion among the Christian churches can become an abstraction. These essays, however, give a solid and experiential basis to the quest on which the church has been embarked for these past thirty-five years.

1

The centrality of a hunger for a common eucharistic table stands central to the spirituality recommended in this volume. Theological agreements serve our pilgrimage together toward that time when Christians can gather around one altar. By linking these ecumenical and eucharistic reflections to the liturgical cycle and the seasons of the year, Father Falardeau has provided important insights that can deepen the understanding and enrich the spiritual life.

In Pope John Paul's 1995 encyclical, *Ut Unum Sint,* we are encouraged: "At the stage [in our journey together as churches] which we have now reached, this process of mutual enrichment must be taken seriously into account...a new task lies before us: that of receiving the results already achieved" which "must involve the whole people of God." Results are not to remain "statements of bilateral commissions but must become a common heritage." This volume will enable the reader to draw on experiences that will make the journey vivid to those who hear these stories and reflections.

Themes of marriage, repentance, Mary, the Holocaust, Jewish High Holy Days, the Reformation, relationships with particular churches, the communion of saints, intermingle with the centrality of the Eucharist, the call to full unity and the elements of the church's year of grace to provide a rich medley of images and aspirations from which to preach and teach and on which to meditate and reflect in the course of the year.

> *Brother Jeffrey Gros, F.S.C.*
> Associate Director
> Secretariat for Ecumenical
>   and Interreligious Affairs
> National Conference of Catholic Bishops

Introduction

This book was in the making for about fifteen years. During that time I contributed regularly to the monthly issues of *People of God,* the newspaper of the Archdiocese of Santa Fe. It was natural that these articles often reflected the liturgical year and the calendar of events that are regularly celebrated by Christians everywhere.

At the suggestion of Fr. Lawrence Boadt, C.S.P., publisher of Paulist Press, I sorted through the articles, arranged them according to topic and placed them in chapters that reflected their original settings. They thus provide reflections for the entire year.

Ecumenism, the movement for Christian unity, is a spirituality (see Vatican Council II, *Unitatis Redintegratio* #8), a world view that sees the scandal of the divisions among Christians, and repents of past sins and present obstacles to the prayer of Jesus "that all may be one..." (Jn 17:21).

Those of us who have labored long at Christian unity and interreligious cooperation know that ecumenism must be local to be real. While the work of ecclesiastical leaders and theologians is important, even more significant is the reception of their work in the lives of people. The Vatican II decree on Christian unity makes it clear that such reception is possible only with a change of mind and heart—a genuine conversion—among the people.

I hope that readers will find in these pages inspiration for spiritual ecumenism and suggestions for practical steps to promote Christian unity. Initially the audience for these reflections was Catholics living in New Mexico. Through careful editing they now address a wider audience and seek a more universal appeal.

I am deeply grateful to Colleen Kilian, my secretary, for the many hours of painstaking secretarial assistance. I thank

Fr. Lawrence Boadt, C.S.P., for his encouragement and suggestions for organizing the material and Donna Crilly, editor, for going over the manuscript and offering useful suggestions.

Albuquerque, NM
December 8, 1999

January

Prayer for Unity

1. Why Pray for Unity?

Why the question? There are many people who feel that getting aboard the ecumenical bandwagon was a mistake, that Vatican II should not have made the move, and that the best thing we can do is to slow down the pace of this movement for unity. Others feel that unity among Christians and between the churches is impossible, and that to pray for such an eventuality is an exercise in frustration. Finally, others see no value in prayer itself. The only thing that happens, they feel, is what human beings do for themselves.

The Value of Prayer

For people of faith, the value of prayer is clear. The gospel tells us to ask and we shall receive. St. Paul frequently speaks of prayer. He especially is confident that the prayer of Jesus will always be answered. Jesus himself said to pray in his name, if we wish to be heard.

Prayer for unity is important because Jesus prayed for it (Jn 17:21). By praying for unity among Christians we are praying with Jesus, and his prayer is always heard. As a matter of fact, the unity of the church is a given. In the Creed we say: I believe in *one,* holy, catholic, and apostolic church. The church is one. Its unity needs only to be recognized and made visible. In fact, Jesus prays that Christians may be one, *so that the world may believe* (Jn 17:21). The importance of praying for unity is that otherwise the world will not believe.

Striving for Unity

Vatican Council II's *Decree on Ecumenism* states:

> Concern for restoring unity pertains to the whole church, faithful and clergy alike. It extends to every one, according to the potential of each....*This very concern already reveals to some extent the bond of brotherhood among all Christians, and leads toward that full and perfect unity which God lovingly desires. [Italics mine]* (*UR* #5)

The very fact that one is concerned about unity and prays for it, the Council says in effect, is the beginning of the ecumenical spirit. This statement reminds us that there are two important effects of prayer. The first is its effect on the one who prays. This effect is infallible (and the reason why we can say that prayers are always answered); namely, it changes the person who prays. The *Decree on Ecumenism* states clearly that those who pray for unity are already undergoing the kind of transformation needed for its realization.

The second effect of prayer relates to the object for which one prays. This object is realized according to God's will. We know that God wants some things to happen because people pray for them to occur. This is part of God's providence. We know that God wants Christian unity. Jesus himself prayed for it (and his prayers are surely answered). To pray for unity is to pray for the accomplishment of God's will.

The Church's Commitment

Another reason why prayer for unity is encouraged is because the church is irrevocably committed to Christian unity. The pope has repeatedly stated that commitment. The time of realization is known to God alone. But from now on the church cannot stop wanting Christian unity. It is clearly God's will, the prayer of Christ and the goal of the church renewed by Vatican II.

The Week of Prayer for Unity is traditionally the time for more than prayer. The Holy Father and other leaders of the ecumenical movement use this week for special gatherings, celebrations, conferences and announcements. For this reason it is a week of prayer and a week of realization of the goal of these prayers. A time of hope and progress, this week should generate much confidence as well. God wills it! It will be done!

2. Ambassadors of Reconciliation

So we are ambassadors for Christ, as if God were appealing through us. We implore you on behalf of Christ, be reconciled to God (2 Cor 5:20). Those who work and pray for Christian unity need the diplomatic qualities and virtues of ambassadors. Their essential task is to reconcile divided parties.

Reconciliation is no easy task. Those who come to the table are divided, hurt and offended. They may be hostile and belligerent. The task of the ambassador is to move the participants to higher ground. He or she must help the negotiators to see the blessing of reconciliation. Nursing the hurts of the past, brooding over wrongs—real or imagined—will only perpetuate the conflict; it will not bring peace to the parties. In modern terms it is possible for both parties to win. But to do so, both must be willing to change.

For our sake he made him to be sin who did not know sin, so that we might become the righteousness of God in him (2 Cor 5:21). St. Paul uses the stark example of Jesus' wanting so much to reconcile us to God that he was even willing to "become sin for our sake." If the sinless Christ was willing to go this far for our reconciliation, how far are we willing to go? What a wonderful model he gives us in our efforts to reconcile.

Pope John Paul II in *Conversion and Evangelization* his encyclicals *Tertio Millennio Adveniente* and in *Ut Unum Sint* stresses the need for conversion and evangelization if we are to move forward on the road to unity. Conversion and evangelization are the major themes of the pope's efforts for the coming years (including the Special Synod for the Americas). Reconciliation is possible if all parties are open to conversion and open to the good news of the gospel. Sin is not the last word. Christ has conquered sin and death, and he can conquer our divisions.

> The approaching end of the second millennium demands of everyone an *examination of conscience* and the promotion of fitting ecumenical initiatives, so that we can celebrate the Great Jubilee, if not completely united, *at least much closer to overcoming the divisions of the second millennium*. As everyone recognizes, an enormous effort is needed in this regard. It is essential not only to continue along the path of dialogue on doctrinal matters, but above all to be more committed to *prayer for Christian unity*. Such prayer has become much more intense after the Council, but it must increase still more, involving an ever greater number of Christians, in unison with the great petition of Christ before his Passion: "Father...that they also may all be one in us." (Jn 17:21) (*TMA* #34)

Many ecumenical observers are pointing out the many bilateral proposals that are coming to maturity at this time as signs of the reconciliation for which Pope John Paul is praying. Anglican-Lutheran, Lutheran-Reformed, Lutheran-Roman Catholic, and (in the U.S.A.) the Council on Church Union agreements have been hammered out in recent years and adopted by a number of churches.

In the final analysis, more than church agreements are needed. The reception of these agreements, that is, the internalization of the ecumenical process by each person, is the measure of the success of the ecumenical movement and the reconciliation it entails.

3. Listen! I Stand at the Door and Knock (Rev 3:14–22)

This passage is taken from the letter to the church at Laodicea found in the third chapter of the Book of Revelation. The message is from Jesus to a church described as *lukewarm*.

> *"So, because you are lukewarm, and neither cold nor hot, I am about to spit you out of my mouth." (Rev 3:16)*

The church at Laodicea is self-sufficient; it is affluent; it is not listening to the Spirit who speaks to the churches. And so Jesus tells the church to above all *listen. "...[L]isten to what the Spirit is speaking to the churches"* (Rev 3:22).

> *"Listen! I am standing at the door, knocking; if you hear my voice and open the door, I will come in to you and eat with you, and you with me."* (Rev 3:20)

What the Lord Jesus proposes is that the church of Laodicea open its doors and let the Lord in. He will come and sup with them. Bach's *Cantata* #61, "Savior of the Nations, Come," interprets the passage thus: "To those (who open the door) I will come in and celebrate the Lord's Supper with them and they with me."

Among the important ideas that have circulated in recent years has been the call of Pope John Paul II for a profound ecumenical effort in the years before the Third Millennium. Almost on cue, a number of churches scheduled important decisions for the coming years.

An agreement to remove the mutual condemnations between Lutherans and Catholics (the anathemas of the Council of Trent) as no longer applicable, is before these churches. Full communion status between Anglicans (U.S.A.) and Lutherans (ELCA), between the Lutheran World Federation and the Federation of Reformed Churches, between the nine denominations (U.S.A.) called the Consultation on Church Union (Episcopal, United Methodist, Presbyterian, American Methodist Episcopal, American Methodist Episcopal Zion, Christian Methodist Episcopal, International Council of Community Churches, United Church of Christ, and Christian Church (Disciples), are all scheduled. Efforts at full communion between the Roman Catholic and Orthodox Churches continue, though without a target date. The relationship between these two churches is considered to be in "almost full communion."

In the light of this reality and the need to implement existing agreements at the local level, our theme—the invitation to open the door—is very timely.

Behold I Stand and Knock

The problem with the church of Laodicea and with the church in our time is that it has become complacent. Lack of zeal, the absence of a sense of urgency, the spark that makes things happen, isn't there. Without the openness to the Spirit and the desire to change, things will remain the same.

Until the pain of separation is felt, there is no compelling need for unity. Unless there is dissatisfaction with the disunity of the churches, there can be no desire for their reconciliation. Without the realization that the church cannot be truly catholic without full communion among all Christians, there can only be a policy of business as usual.

While tremendous progress has been recorded in recent years, ranging from a total change of climate in some places to a wide range of theological breakthroughs (more and more issues are no longer seen as church-dividing), the road to unity still seems a long one. The courage and determination needed to continue the journey rest on openness to the Spirit and willingness to seek God's will in prayer.

Eucharist

The Eucharist is crucial to Christian unity. As often as we "break the bread and drink the cup" we proclaim that the Lord died that "all may be one...so that the world may believe." He came to bring salvation to all, to make one the family of humankind. Salvation and evangelization require the unity of Christians. A world torn by selfishness and pride, by war and division, by exploitation and careless abuse of created resources requires that Christians and all people of faith unite.

A better view of the world is needed. Such a view can only come when all Christians contribute their combined insights and collective wisdom. The world is too small and the problems too large for people to neglect the gifts and talents of all.

4. Communion in God—
Life Together (Jn 15:1-17)

This theme flows directly from the Seventh International Faith and Order Conference which was held in August of 1993 at Santiago de Compostella in Spain. The theme of that conference was *Towards Communion (**Koinonia**) in Faith, Life and Worship.* Since Vatican II the theme of communion/*koinonia* has dominated theological reflection around the nature of the church and Christian unity.

This theme indicates the intimate connection between the communion which we have with God and with one another. As Saint John tells us, the two cannot be separated.

> Whoever does not love does not know God, for God is love. Those who say, "I love God," and hate their brothers or sisters, are liars; for those who do not love a brother or sister whom they have seen, cannot love God whom they have not seen. (1 Jn 4:8 and 20)

The love that binds together the Persons of the Trinity is the love that unites Christians to Christ and to one another. The Body of Christ is united by the Holy Spirit, and Jesus Christ who is head of the Body (Eph 1:22-23).

Communion with God

Cardinal Augustine Bea has continually drawn attention to the common baptism of Christians as the foundation for Christian unity. All those who are baptized in the name of the Father, Son and

Holy Spirit, by one who intends to do what the church does, confers valid baptism.

> Baptism constitutes the foundation of communion among all Christians, including those who are not yet in full communion with the Catholic Church: *"For those who believe in Christ and have been properly baptized are put in some, though imperfect, communion with the Catholic Church...." "Baptism therefore constitutes **the sacramental bond of unity** existing among all who through it are reborn."* [Non-bold italics mine] *(Catechism of the Catholic Church #1271)*

Life Together

The consequence of our communion with God through Christ is that we share life together. This means more than a good feeling among Christians. It is a realization that the communion we share as Christians is intended for the whole human family.

Some visible reality needs to reflect the prayer of Jesus and the ecumenical vision. Visible unity involves a mutual recognition of baptism, Eucharist and ministry. At the level of the diocese and parish, visible unity requires *reception* of agreed statements of the churches and consequent ecumenical activity. Common prayer, social outreach and decision-making to renew individuals, families, communities and culture are ways of uniting Christians.

John 15:1-17

> "I am the true vine, and my Father is the vine grower. He removes every branch in me that bears no fruit. Every branch that bears fruit he prunes to make it bear more fruit....Just as the branch cannot bear fruit by itself unless it abides in the vine, neither can you unless you abide in me." (Jn 15:1-5)

Many of us are not familiar with vine dressing. We are not aware that in winter the growth of the vine is pruned back and only the stalk appears. In spring, as the sap of the vine runs through the stalk it begins to sprout branches, tendrils, twigs and eventually flowers and gives fruit in abundance. This is an apt picture for hope during our *ecumenical winter.*

Santiago's Faith and Order Conference recognized that the unity of Christians is something that is more than "seasonal." It exists because of its foundation in faith in Jesus Christ through baptism. The ups and downs of one church or another cannot destroy the solid foundation upon which the movement for unity exists. It is linked to the flow of love and divine grace through the Body of Christ by the gift of the Holy Spirit.

Prayer continues to be a most important activity of Christians because without it we cannot accept the grace of conversion which we all need to recognize our unity and how we can express it in visible ways.

5. Kindling the Ecumenical Vision

One of the current dangers to the ecumenical movement is complacency and discouragement. It is easy to say that if unity has not come in twenty-five years, it will never come. One can easily slip into a *business-as-usual* attitude.

Without Vision the People Perish

People perish without a vision. They accept injustice, violence, war, poverty, and human degradation. Similarly Christians can (and have) accepted division among themselves for over fifteen hundred years.

The Second Vatican Council has declared that the movement for unity is a gift of the Holy Spirit. This view sharply contrasts with an earlier view that denied any Catholic participation in the movement. Even today there remain those who are suspicious about the goals of the ecumenical movement. Is it another way for the churches to proselytize? Is it a "papering over" of differences to reach some common denominator? What is the vision of Christian unity?

The Vision of Christian Unity

One of the problems we face is the lack of a clear vision of what Christian unity is. It is a gift of the Holy Spirit, but the Spirit does not speak in clear words and concepts. The vision of Christian unity involves a journey. While we have some idea of the goal, the steps along the way are revealed slowly and progressively as we move toward the goal. This idea of gradualism is clearly indicated by Vatican II. There is never a time when we can say "enough." The journey must continue. There must never be a turning back.

Perhaps those who began the ecumenical journey in the halcyon days after Vatican II had the vision of institutional and corporate unity. If everyone agrees, we can readily sweep away our differences and quickly merge into a "super-church." That vision, if it ever existed, was too easy and simple.

The vision of Vatican II was a gradual development of "communion/*koinonia*." This vision continues ever more clearly as the paradigm. The model is the Trinity which is a communion of Father, Son, and Spirit. We enter that communion by the grace and salvation of Jesus Christ. He died for our salvation and rose for our justification. John, in his first Letter tells us:

> What we have seen and heard we proclaim in turn to you so that you may share life with us. This fellowship of ours is with the Father and with his Son, Jesus Christ. (1 Jn 1:3)

The vision of Christian unity today emphasizes the unity of Christians, rather than institutional or structural unity. Obviously the goal is *visible* unity. Unity of faith, unity of worship, and unity in decision making. This implies a unity that is not merely spiritual or ideological.

But such a visible unity is not possible unless it is preceded and accompanied by a recognition of the unity that already exists among all Christians by virtue of their baptism in Jesus Christ and the sharing of a common faith that Jesus Christ is Lord.

Mutual recognition of Christians and mutual respect is at the heart of the ecumenical vision. With such respect and mutual recognition it is possible to see how Christians can give common witness and be engaged in a common mission. In terms of evangelization, the ideal outcome of this vision is that at some point in time we would begin to develop the many possibilities of evangelizing *together*.

Kindling the Vision

The *New Ecumenical Directory* (1993) enlists the collaboration of religious communities in ecumenical ministry, with ecumenical representatives to be named from each religious community. It also suggests that a committee be formed to carry out this task in an orderly and organized fashion.

When the ecumenical vision becomes part and parcel of the fabric of daily life for religious men and women, it will then be possible to "dream the impossible dream" of a Christianity united by God's grace and the work of the Holy Spirit. Living on the cutting edge of the prophetic witness of the church, religious men and women are particularly called to share its vision and the mission to make the gospel real in our time.

6. Called to Be One in Heart and Soul (Acts 4:23–37)

The Acts of the Apostles recalls the unity of the early Christian community. They were one in faith and love. None of their number was in want because everything was shared in common.

> The whole group of believers was united, heart and soul;
> no one claimed for his own use anything that he had, as
> everything they owned was held in common. (Acts 4:32)

This model for the church of every age is a wonderful call for Christians today—a call to be one "in heart and soul," as the early church was.

The New Testament writings indicate that preserving unity was not without its problems then, just as it is now. Paul, in his first letter to the Corinthians, describes the factions that existed in his time: "I am for Paul, I am for Apollos, I am for Peter" were slogans bandied about in the Corinthian community (1 Cor 1:12).

Paul urged his followers to find their unity in the Spirit and the bond of peace, but especially in the Eucharist. "Because the bread is one, we, though many, are one body because we share the one bread" (1 Cor 10:17).

The Eucharist is the foretaste of the heavenly banquet, where the communion of the saints will be perfect, and everlasting. The Eucharist unites us to Christ, to the Father, and to one another. We experience in the Eucharist the unity of the church which will be perfect when the Lord comes again in glory.

Because the early Christian church was made up of eyewitnesses of the resurrection, it is a model for all time of preaching the "good news."

Praying for Unity

The text from Acts reminds us that prayer is a vital part of the Christian community. The early Christians understood that everything in the line of grace is God's gift. They had personally experienced their own conversion from doubt to faith, from infidelity to fidelity. Since everything depends on God, they turned to God in their need.

> ...And now, Lord, take note of their threats and help your servants to proclaim your message with all boldness, by stretching out your hand to heal and to work miracles and marvels through the name of our servant Jesus. As they prayed, the house where they were assembled rocked; they were all filled with the Holy Spirit and began to proclaim the word of God boldly. (Acts 4:29-31)

We should follow their example of prayer and proclamation in our time. Though the movement for Christian unity may have lost some of its enthusiasm, it has not lost its rationale. Nor has it lost the dedication of theologians and others who promote Christian unity. Nor is the commitment of the church to unity waning.

Church unity is more a matter of recognition than of creation. Unity is God's gift. Indeed it is something already given. We are united in Christ by our baptism. We need to acknowledge the various degrees of communion which exist among all Christians. Such recognition should lead us to work and pray for still greater openness to each other.

Working for Unity

The early Christian community did more than pray together. They worked together. They shared their goods and their lives. No one was in want because all shared what they had. Those who love Christ and worship God must work for a better world and a better distribution of the world's riches. The moral implications of receiving the Body of Christ in the Eucharist are that we must "put on the mind of Christ" and reach out to all those marginalized by our society: the poor, the lame, the blind, the sinful.

The question that surfaces at this time of year is "what can I do?" Everyone can pray. Many can contribute financially to the work of ecumenical organizations. Each of these organizations is involved in social outreach at the local, national and international level in an ecumenical spirit.

Each of us can become better informed about the work of the church in the ecumenical field. This work is going on similarly at the level of the parish, diocese, nation and church. This work is both theological, pastoral and practical. Everyone can be involved; there is something for everyone to do.

7. "Remember, I Am with You Always..." (Mt 28:19–20)

Currently there is much discussion of religion and culture throughout the world. The quincentennial of the coming of Europeans to the Americas has been the focus for this discussion. After five hundred years of history, we look at what happened far differently than those who lived through those early years and eras. We recognize that there were both gifts and burdens given to peoples of various cultures. Religious heritage was often trampled rather than respected. Some religious beliefs and practices were imposed rather than proposed.

Exploitation of peoples, lands, and resources even now continues to take place. There are bitter memories to heal. There are wrongs and injustices to be righted, and prejudices and stereotypes to be eradicated. A teachable moment is now available—an opportunity and a challenge. We can learn from the past. We can seize the opportunity. We can accept the challenge.

"I Will Be with You..."

God is with us forever. He is with us in our struggle and in our triumph. In our pain and sinfulness, God sustains us and forgives us. In our moments of grace and accomplishments he gives his Spirit and enables us to creatively build his kingdom. We worship the God of history, the God who created the world and sent his Son to redeem and transform it. God is with us on our journey to the heavenly kingdom.

The God of history is never absent from it. He is with the human race in its most glorious moments and in its most sinful times. He has given human beings the power and responsibility to choose. He does not take back the freedom given. God gives both the power and the decision. He sustains us in our good deeds and our evil acts.

God is especially with us in the Eucharist. Jesus Christ is our companion *(cum panis)*. He breaks bread with us so that we can feel his presence in our pain, and the surge of risen life in our joy.

We celebrate the accomplishments of the past five hundred years. We mourn the tragic errors of this era as well.

8. Praise the Lord All Nations

Hallelujah. Praise God All You Peoples (Ps 117) invites all the nations of the world and all peoples to praise God. This is the shortest of all the psalms, and one of the most beautiful.

> Praise the Lord, all you nations;
> glorify him, all you peoples!
> For steadfast is his kindness toward us,
> and the fidelity of the Lord endures forever. (Ps 117)

We often think of prayer as petition. We need something. Even if our need is spiritual (God's grace, our forgiveness), we are the focus of this kind of prayer. Prayer of praise and thanksgiving (the Jewish term is the same for both: *berakah*) focuses on God and our relationship to him. Psalm 117 contains expressions of both praise and thanksgiving. The reason we praise God is his kindness toward us, and his fidelity. Faith and hope are interwoven into the fabric of this psalm. God's love for us and our response of love are also implied. A perfect prayer!

Since 1908, Christians have been praying together for the unity of all Christian churches. In many ways these prayers have been answered, even though full communion between all Christians remains to be achieved. A new climate of recognition and cooperation hastens the day when Christians may share the Eucharist together–one goal of the ecumenical movement.

The Importance of Prayer

The Second Vatican Council underscored the importance of prayer in its document on ecumenism *(Unitatis Redintegratio)* as crucial to the success of its efforts. The church recognizes that Christian unity is not a human achievement. So many things have divided Christians for so long that healing the wounds and reconciling people is beyond human measures. Hence the importance of prayer.

Prayer prepares us and changes our attitudes and ideas so that we can receive the grace of unity to which God calls us. The decree on ecumenism calls Christian unity "the work of the Holy Spirit" and says that every Christian is being called to the change of heart and mind which are required so that unity may be possible.

Christian unity is God's work, but it is also our own. We need to work and pray. Theological dialogue is needed to remove age-old obstacles to unity. Programs of education and cooperation are needed so that Christians can come to know one another and learn from each other. Working side by side with other Christians is an important way of coming to appreciate others.

Praising God Together

Praising God together seems especially appropriate for an ecumenical setting. It is an affirmation of our common faith and the hope we share as Christians. Whatever our differences in the confession of our faith, we believe that God saves us in Jesus Christ. We believe in the communion *(koinonia)* of saints—that we are united in Christ on earth and will share eternal life together in heaven. Our praise of God is one with all those who have gone before us believing in Jesus Christ as Savior. Our praise is joined to that of the heavenly hosts and the "saints of old" in heaven.

Week of Prayer

The Week of Prayer for Christian Unity is traditionally a focus for all kinds of ecumenical activity. But most important of all are the millions of hearts and voices that raise a prayer to God *that all may be one*. That is the prayer of Jesus. It cannot fail to be answered.

9. One Body in Christ

> Just as each of our bodies has several parts and each part
> has a separate function, so all of us, in union with Christ,
> form one body, and as parts of it we belong to each other.
> (Rom 12:4-5)

This is a most appropriate focus for our prayer and ecumenical
effort, not only during the Week of Prayer for Christian Unity, but
for the entire year. What we are doing when we work and pray for
unity is precisely building the community that is the body of Christ.

The most fundamental concept of the church as described in
the Acts of the Apostles and the writings of St. Paul, especially in 1
Corinthians and Ephesians, is communion *(koinonia)*. The gospels
speak first of all of the communion with God of Jesus Christ. He was
in constant communion with the Father and the Holy Spirit. The
Incarnation was the outpouring of the divine life of the Son of God
into the humanity of Jesus of Nazareth. The first "body of Christ" is
the physical body of the man Jesus who is Son of God. The communion between the humanity and divinity of Jesus is the basis for
all other communions between God and humanity. Because the
Word was made Flesh it is possible for all of us to have communion
with God in Christ.

Jesus said: "I am the vine and you are the branches" (Jn 15:5).
Through baptism we achieve *communion* with Christ and in him.
Through the Eucharist this communion in the body of Christ is deep-
ened. The Bread of Life is broken so that we share divine life. The cup
of salvation is "poured out" so that we share in the saving sacrifice of
Christ. Thus we become branches on the vine which is Jesus. Just as he

"has life because of the Father," so we who eat the Bread of life draw life "because of him" (Jn 6:57). This communion in Christ and sharing together as members of his body is the reason why we have *communion* with each other. This is what Paul explains in his various epistles.

Prior to Vatican II, communion in the Body of Christ was something Roman Catholics believed to be theirs exclusively. Other Christians had similar ideas about their own churches, whether Orthodox, Evangelical, or Protestant. People gloried in thinking of themselves as *exclusive* members of the Body of Christ. Indeed our ecclesiology even today suffers from this sense of exclusiveness. Vatican II realized that such an ecclesiology would not be helpful to the development of unity among Christians. Something else was needed. Indeed as theologians searched the scriptures and the writings of the Fathers of the Church, it became clear that this kind of exclusiveness was contrary to the scriptures and the long tradition of the church. Moreover it was not true to the facts.

Many Christians are validly baptized. Many receive the Eucharist from validly-ordained priests. For example, Ancient Eastern and Eastern Orthodox bishops and priests have always been recognized as having valid ordinations and sacraments. As the Vatican Council says in the *Decree on Ecumenism,* these Christians are members of the Body of Christ and in some measure *in communion* with the Catholic Church. The ecumenical task is to make that communion more and more *full.* Through dialogue a deeper sharing of faith is developed; through ecumenical cooperation a greater charity is shared; through recognition of ministries and authority a greater hope emerges. Thus the community is built and the Body of Christ develops.

Praying for unity is more than one way of working for it. Prayer for unity is *the most important way* of achieving unity. Worship together is the greatest sign of shared faith, hope and charity. The goal of unity is shared prayer and worship. It is both God's will and God's work. We are very close to the heart of Jesus Christ when we pray with him:

> "I pray not only for these, but for those also who through their words will believe in me. May they be one, Father, may they be one in us, as you are in me and I am in you, so that the world may believe it was you who sent me." (Jn 17:20-21)

February

Unity and Repentance

1. Christians Are Divided: Do We Weep?

Lent is a time for repentance. The word means sorrow for sin. Do we have any sorrow because Christians are divided? Do we feel guilty about these divisions? Lent is a time to reflect about our sorrow for this collective sin and our part in it.

The Second Vatican Council has indicated that the division of Christians cannot be blamed upon existing Christians. It is a little like original sin. It is hard to be sorry about Adam's sin because we aren't responsible for it. But we do share in the responsibility for the division of Christianity. It is largely the guilt of our ancestors. But the continuation of a sinful state of affairs lays this guilt on our doorstep.

What Can Be Done About It?

More important than the repentance we should feel about the continuing division of the church, is what we are doing about it. Pope John Paul II's encyclical *Ut Unum Sint,* and the *Directory for the Application of Principles and Norms on Ecumenism,* suggest a number of ways in which we can move from repentance to action.

The first step is awareness of the divisions and how sinful they are. They are directly opposed to the prayer of Jesus for unity (Jn 17:21ff) and the will of God. This does not mean that God wants uniformity. He wants unity in diversity. Our problem is accepting the diversity that God wills for his church.

The second step is a study of scripture. The word of God is the revelation of God's will for us. The scriptures teach us God's mercy and love. From Jesus Christ we learn to forgive those who hate us; we learn to love all as brothers and sisters in Christ.

A third step is dialogue. Dialogue is a discipline. It is a conversation in which trust grows and develops because those who engage in it do so as equals. The greatest obstacle to dialogue is a sense of superiority or a sense of inferiority. At the table of dialogue (Christian and interreligious) each person has equal dignity as a child of God.

A final step is personal commitment. The encyclical of John Paul II and the Directory on Ecumenism indicate that the Catholic church is *irrevocably* committed to the unity of all Christians. It calls upon bishops, clergy, and the laity to be equally committed to the unity of the church.

Unity among Catholics

One of the greatest obstacles to unity among Christians is the internal divisions of Christians within their own church. It is quite evident that Catholic Christians are not united. Though they share faith, sacraments, scripture, and tradition, Catholic Christians have been terribly polarized during the time since the Second Vatican Council. This is understandable. There are those who think the Council went too far, and those who think it did not go far enough. Conservative and liberal elements in the church were able to come together at the Council, but in the aftermath they have continued to drift apart.

Perhaps what is needed is a Third Vatican Council. In the meantime, Catholic Christians need to feel the pain of their divisions and ask God for forgiveness and for the grace to move toward greater unity. As they draw closer to Christ, Catholic Christians will draw closer to Christians of other churches and denominations.

It Takes Time

In the past quarter century since Vatican Council II, an extraordinary amount of progress has been made toward Christian unity. The atmosphere today is dramatically different from what it was in the 1940s and 1950s. The ecumenical movement has touched every church and every Christian. But there is much more to be done. Organic and lasting change does not come easily. It takes time.

Since the Council, theologians and hierarchs in ecumenical dialogue have paved the way for the unity of the churches. What remains is the great task of *reception* of this progress by rank and file Christians. Reception in its technical and ecumenical sense means the assimilation into the mainstream of life of the decisions reached in ecumenical dialogue.

While these dialogues have received official responses, they have not yet been popularly accepted. People continue to live their lives in the same way. When daily life, spirituality, liturgy, and other aspects of church life are affected by the ecumenical spirit, then true reception will have taken place.

Nevertheless, some progress in reception has been achieved. The greatest evidence of it is in liturgy. The texts read at services have been chosen, arranged and translated by experts ecumenically. Liturgical formulas resemble one another.

Lent is a time of repentance. It is a time for spring growth and renewal. For Christians, I suggest, it is a time to weep over our collective sin of division as well as our personal sins of commission and omission. With such repentance will come God's grace of forgiveness and amendment—the grace of greater unity in Christ.

2. Lent, Repentance and Christian Unity

Lent brings into focus several dimensions of Christian unity. Christians celebrate the season of Lent. For centuries Lent has been an important part of the spiritual life of Orthodox, Catholics, Anglicans and Lutherans, and many other Christians. Today, thanks to the Second Vatican Council and the liturgical and biblical renewals that have touched every Christian church, Lent is an important time of spiritual renewal and profound reflection for virtually all Christians. And so it is an ideal time to reflect upon Christian unity.

A Time of Repentance

Lent is a time of repentance. Christians recognize their individual and corporate sinfulness. Since Vatican II we are more conscious that God saves us and deals with us as a people as well as individually. We are more aware of corporate sin. Such sin results from the exploitation of people, and from our negligence to improve the lot of millions in our country and throughout the world. Liberation theology has sensitized the northern and western hemispheres to the plight of those who live in the eastern and southern part of our globe.

Repentance for Disunity

We are guilty of personal sins. We are also guilty of our tolerance of injustice and disunity. "Whatever you did not do to the least, you did not do for me" (Mt 25:45). Are not our sins of omission far more glaring and ominous than our sins of commission? Have we done everything we can to bring about the unity of Christians "so that the world may believe" (Jn 17:20)? It is very difficult to answer in the affirmative.

Time of Renewal

Lent as a time of renewal should help us to focus on such issues as peace, justice, and the environment. These topics have taken center stage in ecumenical reflections today. The Fifth International Conference on Faith and Order (Santiago, August 1993) made it clear that Christian people need to be more aware of our communion in God. More importantly, we need to ask ourselves how this affects our life together. The fate (and the faith) of millions will depend upon what Christians do to improve the lot of the needy.

Vatican II

The Second Vatican Council urges Catholic Christians to repent (as the Council Fathers did in 1965) for the sins that caused the breakdown of Christianity, East and West, Catholic and Protestant. As the Groupe des Dombes emphasizes (*For the Conversion of the Churches,* 1993), we need a change of heart, a genuine conversion. Such a process involves the grace of God. Grace is never lacking, but human cooperation often is.

During the time of Lent we are more attentive to God speaking through the scriptures, the liturgy and the season. It is a "time of grace." God is generous with grace, and we are more open to cooperate with it.

Time of Prayer

Lent is a time of prayer. We pray for forgiveness of sin; we also pray "deliver us from evil." The evil of disunity must be recognized, repented and repaired. Once we understand the evil of division, we grasp the imperative to work for unity. Thus we can improve our attitude toward other Christians, and celebrate with them the Easter of Christ's joyful triumph over sin and death.

3. Ecumenical Activities for Lent

How can we promote Christian unity? Lent offers many wonderful opportunities. Some of these activities include: joint Ash Wednesday Services, Palm Sunday Services, Good Friday "Tre Ore" (Three Hours) Services, and Easter Sunrise Services. These can be tailored to the local situation. It can be as simple as offering blessed ashes to a Protestant neighbor, or inviting him or her to our church for ashes. It can be giving blessed ashes to a Protestant minister who doesn't have the blessing of ashes in his or her ritual.

Some of the parishes have been joining for years for the blessing of palms on Palm Sunday. After the palms are blessed, each congregation processes to its respective church. Ecumenical Tre Ore Services on Good Friday are a long-standing tradition.

Catholics are not used to having sunrise services on Easter. However, Protestants have been doing them ecumenically for many years. Catholics are most welcome. Since no eucharist is involved, it is a readily available opportunity for sharing in prayer across church lines.

A number of very creative programs during Lent exist. The one that impressed me most was a Lenten supper each Wednesday evening at which soup, bread, and little or no dessert are eaten. This Lenten meal provides the opportunity to donate the financial savings to a favorite or combined charity. After the meal the congregations gather at one of the churches for an ecumenical service. This is sometimes a Eucharist. At the service one of the priests or pastors speaks on a subject of common or ecumenical interest. Some parishes have an ongoing "sister-church" relationship. They work out various programs throughout the year. During Lent programs for Bible study and other sharing are planned.

Resources

The Graymoor Ecumenical Institute (475 Riverside Drive #528, New York, NY 10115) has published an inexpensive resource: *Local Ecumenism and Interfaith Cooperation* (rev. ed. 1985). It is a treasure of ideas, a bibliography, and contacts through which to develop a year-round program for ecumenical and interfaith cooperation.

Among some of the activities suggested by the Graymoor Institute are lay organizations exchanges, open house programs, interchurch and interfaith prayer services, speaker exchange programs, programs for interchurch and interreligious marriage, joint library facilities, Bible studies, ecumenical dialogue, and covenants between parishes.

Social Action

In addition to sharing prayer, parishes can join together with other Christians and people of faith in social action. Common concerns for the neighborhood can be discussed and appropriate action taken. Lent is a wonderful time to join others in such collaboration.

Problems

Joint activities and ecumenical prayer are not without problems. (Is there anything worth doing that doesn't have problems?) Catholic parishes have overwhelming numbers, often ten times more than their Protestant neighbors in many populated areas. Yet at this time, because Catholics are new at ecumenism, attendance often balances out. Protestants are very willing to join their Catholic neighbors and appreciate the invitation to do so.

Eucharistic sharing is a problem if the prayer service takes on a liturgical form. Yet other forms of worshiping together are readily available (e.g., a service of the Word, with readings, psalms, singing, etc.). If the Eucharist is decided upon, following diocesan ecumenical guidelines will be important.

4. Ethics and Ecumenism

Little attention has been given to a recent document of the Second Anglican-Roman Catholic International Commission entitled *Life in Christ: Morals, Communion and the Church* (1994). But the existence of this document and its content are of great importance.

The Second Vatican Council decree on ecumenism, *Unitatis Redintegratio,* expressed the hope that moral issues might be first on the agenda for dialogue between the churches. At the international level, this wish was not fulfilled—until now. Most of the many dialogues at that level have been on the doctrinal topics which have divided the churches since the Reformation.

Life in Christ is welcome for many reasons. First of all, it moves the dialogue between Anglicans and Roman Catholics beyond the problems of women's ordination and that of recognizing Anglican orders. These "obstacles" seem insurmountable to some. To seasoned ecumenists they are simply obstacles to be surmounted. If Christian unity is the goal, then nothing is insurmountable.

Second, this document moves the dialogue into the important area of Christian morality. For many Christians the disagreement about moral issues is more "church dividing" than issues concerning doctrine. *Life in Christ* makes it clear this is not the case. One of the important points made by this agreed statement is that moral issues do not divide the Church of Rome from the Church of Canterbury.

The rationale behind this statement is that Anglicans and Catholics basically agree when it comes to sources of moral judgment, methods of reaching conclusions, and general principles deduced from this process. Scripture, tradition, reason (theology), and teaching authority are clearly recognized as the sources for moral judgments. While magisterium is more clearly articulated in the Catholic Church, authority for teaching by Anglican bishops is recognized in Anglicanism as well.

As for methodology, moral theology is a science in both communions. *Life in Christ* recognizes that there is little disagreement about major principles derived from the Christian sources used by both churches.

Disagreement is generally in the area of specific moral issues about which there is controversy. However, these differences are not and need not be "church dividing." Indeed, it is acknowledged there is probably as much disagreement about these specific conclusions within the churches as between them.

Freedom of Conscience

One of the great breakthroughs of Vatican II is the document on religious freedom, *Dignitatis Humanae,* which emphasizes the role of conscience in the life of every human being. No one can be forced to believe or to do something against the judgment of conscience. While each person has the obligation to "enlighten" his or her conscience through study of sources, tradition, teaching of the magisterium, and theologians, in the final analysis conscience is the last frontier of human responsibility.

People can more readily understand freedom of conscience in matters of faith. But the same freedom exists in matters of ethics. This is the underlying principle for the church's support of conscientious objection. While in the past the church tended to sustain the obligation of citizens to come to the defense of their country, recent documents make it clear the church recognizes the right to general and specific conscientious objection.

Recent Encyclicals

The content of *Life in Christ* may be compared to two recent encyclicals of Pope John Paul II treating on moral questions. *Veritatis Splendor* and *Evangelium Vitae* were issued to establish a general framework for considering moral issues (VS) and a specific treatment of life and death questions (EV) concerning abortion, contraception, euthanasia and capital punishment.

Both these documents go beyond the scope of the moral issues treated in *Life in Christ*. And for that reason there are some particular differences that will need to be worked out. Perhaps, as with the ARCIC I *Final Report,* these discrepancies could be worked out in "elucidations." Such elucidations would provide the framework for spelling out points of agreement and disagreement.

Dialogue

Pope John Paul II in *Ut Unum Sint* has this to say on the subject of dialogue:

> If prayer is the "soul" of ecumenical renewal and of the yearning for unity, it is the basis and support for everything the council defines as *dialogue*....The capacity for dialogue is rooted in the nature of the person and his dignity....Dialogue is an indispensable step along the path toward human self-realization, the self-realization both of each individual and of every human community. (*UUS* #28)

Dialogue requires mutual respect. And this is true both for matters of faith and for moral matters. One must be able to respect the other person's search for truth. One must believe in the integrity of those who disagree with us.

The Acts of the Apostles (chapter 15) shows how the early church handled disagreements concerning circumcision and other elements of Jewish law. After consultation, the church decided that, because one is justified by faith in Jesus Christ, no requirements of Mosaic Law would be required of Gentile converts to Christianity. For the sake of peace and harmony, the Gentiles were merely asked to observe certain practices concerning meat sacrificed to idols.

Dialogue is the road to truth. Lock-step compliance to authoritarian decisions has left a long trail of human misery from the tortures of the Inquisition to the Nazi holocaust.

5. Costly Unity and Costly Commitment

There is a growing interest in discussion on ethical questions in ecumenical circles. Ethics and morality divide more than Christians; they divide the whole world.

World Council of Churches

The World Council of Churches focuses this issue very clearly. In two studies entitled *Costly Unity* and *Costly Commitment,* the WCC has reported its findings. These two studies are part of an overall analysis of ethics/morality and Christian unity.

For the first time in its history, Division I and Division III of the World Council (Unity and Renewal, together with Justice, Peace and the Integrity of Creation) have joined to study the relationship between ethics and unity. The World Council realizes that without collaboration in the important area of morality it cannot advance the cause of Christian unity.

The study on *Costly Unity* was made at Ronde in Denmark shortly after the International Faith and Order Conference at Santiago de Compostella in Spain (1993). This study finds the cost of unity involves the great moral issues of our day.

The second study group met at Tantur near Jerusalem in 1995 and wrote *Costly Commitment*. Its major insight is that Christian unity requires a commitment to moral issues and moral formation from all Christian churches. The latter point was especially emphasized by Dr. Larry Rasmussen in a paper on the role of the churches in ethical formation. It is the subject of the third and final study in this series.

This last point deserves some attention. *Costly Commitment* discovered that the churches were reluctant to enter into discourse on the moral issues. Too often preaching avoids the burning ethical issues of the day because of their divisive nature. "Let sleeping dogs lie" seems to characterize the attitude of many preachers.

Rasmussen said that the churches must be involved in moral discourse, but also in ethical formation of the people. This is vital in order to emerge from the present problem of disunity in the church. Until all Christians are able to agree and face the disintegrating forces of secularism, moral decay and relativism, the unity of the church is problematic.

Catholic Moral Formation

The World Council of Churches continues to work on moral formation. The shape it will take awaits further study. But already we can see the value of these insights for Catholics. Evidently divisions exist within the church as well as between the churches. The great moral issues of our day need to be faced together. This does not mean that the solution is compromise. Between compromise and rigid immobility there is ample room for mutual enlightenment and a common growth in understanding. This growth in understanding of the complexity of the world in which we live is part of the underlying task of the ecumenical movement. This is the fertile area of ethical formation.

R. Scott Appleby in an article for *Christian Century* ("Crunch Time for American Catholics") pleads "for greater unity through open communication—through listening and speaking to one another in mutual respect and without fear of reprisal. Such communication, it is hoped, will become the essential Catholic *practice* of the new millennium."

If the unity of Christians is predicated on ethical/moral discourse, Catholics must be able to engage in it with civility and respect for one another. Only then can they contribute to the necessary moral formation required in our time.

March

Easter Joy and Christian Unity

1. Easter Joy and Christian Unity

Easter joy and the return of spring renew both nature and our life in Christ. We welcome them and their power to give us new life and vigor. Life is dreary without joy. Indeed it is hardly liveable.

Survivors from gulags and prisoner of war camps point to the absolute necessity of a sense of humor, an ability to retain inner peace and joy in the midst of adversity. Without the ability to see beyond the immediate drama and calamity one cannot survive or live.

This is why Easter is such an important feast. Even more than Christmas, which celebrates the birth of Christ, Easter is necessary for Christians. If Jesus had merely shared our life, we would still have sadness. How could we hope? But Jesus shared our death; indeed through his resurrection he triumphed over the grave.

The joy of Easter is more than a sense of humor. "Life is not ended but merely changed." With the Eastern churches we sing: "Christ is risen! Indeed he is risen!" And that makes all the difference in the world. Easter brings with it a deep and lasting joy.

Ecumenical Sense of Humor

It is easy to lose one's sense of humor. Young and old find life now more difficult to live. There is more violence in our surroundings, less care and more selfishness. People can easily be discouraged if they look only at the problems that face them.

For those who see in the Eucharist a challenge to Christian unity, there is also a danger of losing one's sense of hope. Obstacles to unity continue to emerge, even as greater agreement on matters of morality and doctrine are hammered out. Controversial topics arise to divide Christians at every turn. Is unity among Christians at all possible?

Many believed that the unity of the church would be accomplished in a generation after Vatican II. This has not happened. It is not a matter of ill will. The task was simply much greater than people expected, the obstacles more insurmountable than imagined.

Eucharist

Jesus prayed for unity at the very table at which he instituted the Eucharist. And the Eucharist is a celebration of Easter, of the death and rising of the Lord. The joy of the resurrection keeps us smiling and hoping. As we remember and proclaim the death and rising of the Lord, we remember that we share his joy and will share his glory. Our task is to remember, to celebrate, to believe. We know that his kingdom will come. Our efforts are important to that achievement. Our success in making the unity of Christians visible and palpable depends on God's grace as well as our efforts.

Easter renews our joy and our hope. We celebrate the death and rising of the Lord of glory. In the Eucharist we share the joy and communion of God's kingdom as we remember his Easter triumph over death. If Christ could conquer death, he can surely conquer our divisions.

2. The Cross and the Resurrection

Holy Week and Easter are the celebration of the cross and the resurrection of Jesus Christ. Why it was necessary for the Son of God to die "for us and for our salvation" will always remain a mystery. As St. Paul describes that term, a mystery is the hidden plan of God. Because God is infinite, the depth and breadth of his mind can never be fathomed. Nor can the reasons for his actions.

Reading the scriptures, especially Philippians 2:5-11, we are told that the Son did not cling to divine dignity but humbled himself, accepting a human existence and the humiliation of the cross. Therefore God exalted him, because he was obedient "unto death."

God was not pleased with death, but with the obedience of his Son. On the Second Sunday of Lent, year B, we were reminded of the obedience of Abraham who reluctantly, but obediently, prepared to sacrifice his son Isaac at God's command. Because of this obedience, God created a covenant between Abraham and all his descendants.

The cross remains a mystery. Paul calls it "the power of God" (1 Cor 1:18). The inspiration of Jesus accepting the cross is, for Christians, the powerful incentive to live through the sufferings of life, "...filling up in my body what is wanting to the sufferings of Christ Jesus for the sake of his body, the church" (Col 1:24).

Resurrection

The other side of the coin of Christian faith is the Resurrection. It is the final outcome of the cross. Good Friday leads to Easter Sunday, the empty tomb and the triumph of Christ over death.

"We are resurrection people and *Alleluia* is our song" (Augustine). Christians are not morbid people focused on suffering. They are joyful people centered on the Resurrection.

Life is a bittersweet reality. We have many joys. We also share in the sufferings of life. There are disappointments, physical ills, psychological problems, hardships of all kinds. Through them all there is a realization that life is a gift, that Jesus, Mary, Joseph, and all the saints shared in full measure life's sufferings and sorrows. Yet their peace and joy remained even in the midst of suffering—like sunshine through the rain.

Easter is as welcome as spring. It is the season of joy and hope. The long winter night is over, we greet the brightness of day and the season of promise. Hope springs eternal as we celebrate the central reality of our faith: Christ is risen! Christ will come again!

United in Faith and Communion

Christians around the world share together this central mystery of our faith. They believe that Jesus Christ is the Son of God who came into this world for our salvation. For us he died on a cross. But for our justification he rose from the grave and is the cause of our hope and joy. Orthodox, Catholic, Anglican, Lutheran, Evangelical, Reformed, and Methodist believers all share faith in this central Christian mystery.

In the Eucharist of Easter we "remember" and share not only the "bread and cup," but the very mystery of salvation: the memorial of the passion, death and resurrection of Jesus. We take part in the hope of final glory by sharing the Bread of Life. We join in the eternal prayer of Jesus by being united to the Son of God "ever living to make intercession for us" (Heb 7:25). This is the reason for Easter hope and for Easter joy.

3. Easter and Christian Unity

The Lord is Risen! Alleluia! Throughout all of Christendom this song of joy echoes in every church and every clime. Easter is a common celebration of our faith in Jesus Christ as the Son of God who rose from the dead. His victory over sin and death were complete. On the cross he died for our sins; in the grave he conquered death for our resurrection. All Christians celebrate this same faith and this same feast, even though in a church divided.

A Common Feast

While it may seem obvious that all Christians celebrate the feast of Easter, it is important that we are conscious of the fact. Indeed one of the reasons Christians are divided is because they emphasize points of division rather than elements of agreement.

In this respect all Christians share a common belief that Jesus Christ is the Son of God who died for our sins and rose for our justification and resurrection. The central dogma we believe together is that Jesus Christ is our Lord and Savior.

The joy of Easter is a joy we share in common with all Christians. This joy will ring out on Easter morning in every Christian church, Protestant as well as Catholic. Eastern Christians have a profound sense of the importance of this feast. They celebrate Easter Monday and Tuesday, and continue the celebration throughout the remainder of the week.

Protestant Christians also understand that Easter is central and the most important feast of the year. We owe many of our favorite hymns to them (as they owe many of theirs to the Gregorian melodies of the ancient church).

Catholic Christians find great joy in the celebration of this feast. It is at the heart of our Catholic faith. Though Christmas may have more popular appeal in our church, Easter has a very profound spiritual impact.

Easter and Culture

Our culture has dehumanized human life by its failure to appreciate the precious gift of life and the dignity of each human being. It hardly appreciates the meaning of the Resurrection. It can only understand life as continuing or ceasing. That life should be changed into eternal and divine life is beyond its grasp. The meaning of Easter is, at least in part, that there is a world beyond what we can see and touch. It is the world of the spirit that endures beyond the grave.

Easter is a proof of God's infinite love:

> For God so loved the world that he gave his only Son, so that everyone who believes in him may not perish but may have eternal life. (Jn 3:16)

In a sinful world we know sin did not have the last word. Our sins were nailed to the cross. Death did not conquer. Christ rose from the grave, and we are destined to share the life of the Risen Lord.

Easter and the Eucharist

The Eucharist is the sign of our faith and our celebration of the Paschal Mystery.

> For as often as you eat this bread and drink this cup, you proclaim the Lord's death [and his resurrection] until he comes. (1 Cor 11:26)

Just as Christ overcame sin and death, he will overcome the sin of division which plagues the church and prevents the fullness of its witness. We make this prayer as we celebrate the Eucharist, just as Jesus made his prayer for unity at the Last Supper:

> "... that they may all be one. As you, Father, are in me and I am in you, may they also be in us, so that the world may believe that you have sent me." (Jn 17:21)

We pray that all who celebrate the Paschal Mystery in the Eucharist may rediscover their unity in the Risen Lord.

Pentecost: The Holy Spirit and Unity

1. Pentecost and Prayer

Abbé Couturier of Lyons, France, inaugurated a week of prayer for Christian unity in the 1930s. This week or "octave" of prayer, as it was originally called, was celebrated between the Feast of the Ascension and Pentecost. The apostles prayed during the first "octave" for the birth of the church through the coming of the Holy Spirit. What more appropriate time for prayer today for the unity of the church and the "new Pentecost" envisaged by the Second Vatican Council?

Vatican II entitled its decree on ecumenism *Unitatis Redintegratio,* the re-integration of unity. In the mind of the Council Fathers unity is not something to be created. It is something to be recognized and reintegrated. The church of Christ is one, but divided. The divisions in the church are the result of historical conflicts and differences. The reasons for many of these divisions no longer exist.

For example, in 1985 the Lutheran-Roman Catholic Dialogue in the United States published a study on Justification by Faith. Catholics and Protestants agree that one is justified by grace in faith. The dispute is over. There is a proposal before the Lutheran and Catholic Churches that by the year 2000 the mutual condemnations of the Augsburg Confession (Lutheran) and the Council of Trent (Catholic) be rescinded. The reason for this action is that the condemnations no longer apply—in other words, neither Lutherans nor Catholics maintain the positions characteristic of their churches at the time of the Reformation. As a result of years of dialogue, Lutherans and Catholics realize they are closer together than farther apart.

Prayer and Pentecost

We are all aware that Christian unity will be achieved only through prayer. We know the most important prayer has already been made by Jesus Christ on the night before he died: "Father, may they be one as we are one. I in you and you in me, may they be one in us. May they be one so that the world will believe that you sent me" (Jn 17:21).

Every Christian prayer is made "in the name of Jesus Christ." Our prayer will be heard because Jesus is always heard. When two or three are gathered in his name, Jesus is in our midst. We know that the Holy Spirit is the one who prays in us when we pray to the Father. He prays without words, but with a depth that is beyond human capacity. The Holy Spirit is the bond of love, uniting all the members of the Body of Christ. The Holy Spirit is given to us at baptism and is the binding force of Christian unity. How appropriate, then, to pray to the Holy Spirit on Pentecost and the days preceding it, for a renewal of the church, a "new Pentecost" in our time.

For the last few years at Pentecost, the Archdiocese of Santa Fe, New Mexico, has celebrated an important ecumenical gathering for prayer involving Lutherans, Anglicans (Episcopalians), and Roman Catholics. These three churches "in the catholic tradition" believe they are especially close. Thanks to a generation of dialogue, major obstacles to Christian unity have been eliminated (see The ARCIC *Final Report* and Lutheran World Federation-Roman Catholic *Facing Unity*.) Progress needs to continue.

More importantly the theological unity achieved through dialogue needs to be "received" and appropriated by the people in the pews. This task of *reception* is the most important process needed in the coming years (see John Paul II, *Ut Unum Sint* # 80–81).

Ancient stereotypes and prejudices must give way to a genuine conviction of the unity of all Christians through faith and baptism. This unity must find visible and concrete expression in the way Christians unite to give witness to their common faith in the gospel of Jesus Christ.

2. Bearing the Fruit of the Spirit

The fruit of the Spirit is love, joy, peace, patience, kindness, generosity, faithfulness, gentleness and self-control. (Gal 5:22-23)

In the letter to the Galatians, after describing the "fruits of the flesh" that tear at both the individual and the community, Paul describes the virtues given by the Spirit that build up the Body of Christ and each Christian.

The Graymoor Ecumenical Institute, which prepares Week of Prayer for Christian Unity material distributed throughout the world, indicates that a theme was developed from this text by the people of Zaire (now the Democratic Republic of Congo). They experienced unusual efforts to bring about unity among Christians in their land, which is ninety-five percent Christian. The government of President Mobutu decreed that all Protestant churches in Zaire should become one united Protestant church. One year later the government, in the Law on the Practice of Religion of 1971, formalized its recognition of just four Christian confessions: the Roman Catholic Church, the Orthodox Church, the Church of Christ on Earth, and the Church of Christ in Zaire (one hundred Protestant denominations grouped together). Whether this religious experiment will have lasting fruit remains to be seen.

The church in the Third World, especially in Africa, is making giant strides toward Christian unity. And as we pray for unity among all Christians we take a moment to evaluate progress in other parts of the world.

There are some who believe that the Church of England's decision to ordain women spells the end of the ecumenical movement. But the Episcopal Church in the U.S.A. has been ordaining women since 1976. Lutherans have been ordaining women even longer, and other churches have done so for a century. The ecumenical movement continues. How it will solve these problems remains to be seen, but the challenge of Christ is to unity: "May they be one...so that the world may believe that you love them...and you sent me..." (Jn 17:21 ff).

Rather than look at the obstacles to unity, we should look at the progress made. At Canberra in 1991, the World Council of Churches looked deeply into the relationship between religion and culture. While there was some painful reaction to the subject, the fruits of that discussion continue to enrich the ecumenical movement.

In August, 1993, the Fifth Faith and Order Conference was held at Santiago de Compostella, Spain. Theologians had been working on the theme "Toward Koinonia (Communion) in Faith, Life and Witness." All hope that the kind of progress made at Montreal in 1963 would be repeated. Santiago was both a point of arrival and a point of departure. Progress made will lead to further improvement.

The Week of Prayer for Christian Unity is a time to give thanks and to pray for continued progress. It is an opportunity to inquire about what is going on in your parish to promote the unity to which the church is committed and the fruits of the Spirit lead. It is a time to rededicate ourselves to prayer and work so that Christians may be one, even if the shape of visible unity remains unknown for the moment.

3. Waiting for the Winds

The secular and religious press were quick to headline Dr. Albert Outler's comment that official ecumenism was "dead in the water." (Dr. Outler was speaking to the Major Superiors of Men gathered in St. Louis, Missouri, August 10–14, 1986.) They were not as quick to pick up the context of his remarks, namely, that the ecumenical movement owed a great deal to men and women religious who, in spite of the church's initial coolness to the ecumenical movement, prophetically saw the need to respond to this movement of the Spirit. Outler was calling again on religious orders and their leaders to take up and make their own the challenge of Vatican II to make Christians one.

The unity of the church is not of man's doing, it is God's gift. It will come as a result of prayer and of personal conversion within the church. Spiritual ecumenism is, therefore, paramount. Just as there are structures that sustain injustice and oppress the poor in the world, so there are prejudices and structures that prevent Christian unity. Prayer and work are needed to change these structures into instruments of unity, rather than continuing disunity.

If Outler is right and ecumenism is "dead in the water," then we must pray for the "mighty winds of God" to move us "out into the deep." Ecumenists agree that there is need for a new effort in ecumenism. They do not agree that ecumenism in any sense is dead. They emphasize that if the vertical movement has reached a level when movement seems either to have stopped or no longer to be possible, then a greater effort at horizontal progress is needed.

Dr. George Lindbeck, professor of theology at Yale Divinity School and co-chair of the International Lutheran-Catholic Dialogue, suggests that the Agreed Statement "Facing Unity" (Lutheran World Federation, 1985) is a plan for the development of such horizontal ecumenism. He suggests we must focus on the local church (diocese) and develop a common ecumenical spirituality as the way to insure progress in Christian unity.

This view is encouraging for those persons and places now engaged in bilateral and multilateral dialogue and in efforts at mutual cooperation. It also suggests that future growth in ecumenism will be one of depth rather than breadth. The local church is now, more than ever, the focus of ecumenical development.

4. Sister Churches in Eastern Europe

Developments in Eastern Europe have caught the attention of everyone. Nightly reports of ethnic cleansing in Yugoslavia, and the horror of people being killed even by their own for propaganda purposes, chills even the most stolid. For those following the impact of these events on Christian and interreligious dialogue, there is a certain frustration over people returning to old habits and ways of settling differences.

The ecumenical movement is a new phenomenon. It grew with great difficulty under the communist regime. All religion was suspect and humiliated. The return to "normalcy" is relative. Complex questions such as the return of church property to Catholics in the Ukraine and collaboration between Orthodox and Catholic hierarchies are very delicate matters. Rather than surprise at the lack of total success, one should marvel that any progress is possible at all.

One of the important recent events was the meeting of all the patriarchs of the Orthodox Churches in March of 1992. Their joint communique was unprecedented. The statement made it clear they intend to think and work together, and speak with one voice. They had harsh criticisms for Rome and for the proselytizing of Evangelicals on territory considered to be the private turf of Orthodoxy. One of the principal differences with the Vatican was the appointment of Latin Rite bishops for Moscow and remote areas of Siberia. The Vatican's response was that it was simply answering the needs of people—largely refugees from World War II—in those areas.

Sister Churches

In the Bellamand Agreed Statement, the Orthodox-Catholic Dialogue reaffirmed the importance of viewing each of the participant churches as "Sister Churches." Each is to be treated as an equal partner and the integrity of each is to be maintained and respected. The Agreed Statement flatly rejects "uniatism" as the model for the reconciliation of Rome and the East. The working model for the future is that of communion/*koinonia;* that is, that the church is a communion of those who believe in Jesus Christ. The divided church must be reunited by a greater realization of the basic unity that already exists in the Body of Christ.

What is needed is *renewal,* not reform. At the time of the Reformation and the Council of Trent, the church was in disarray. Reform was required; new structures were needed that would ensure a return to law and order. At the present time legal and structural reform is not a primary concern. The churches can handle their own *aggiornamento.* But the need for renewal, the penetration of gospel values throughout the fabric of the church and society, is clearly a matter of priority.

Beyond Theology and Law

In the new scheme of things the churches must be open to profound change. This is very difficult for the Orthodox Church, which models itself on the Christian Church of the first seven Ecumenical Councils (Nicea to Chalcedon). The Catholic Church has a similar problem because of the enormous influence of the Council of Trent on current doctrinal formulation and canon law. Openness to new formulations and new ways are an integral part of the ecumenical agenda.

For some places this discussion may seem somewhat esoteric. However, the presence of the Orthodox Church (Greek and Russian) and the important developments in understanding emerging from the dialogue require that we continue to keep our eyes on this dialogue and events in Eastern Europe.

5. "We Come To Exchange the Kiss of Christ's Peace"

For those who follow closely ecumenical developments within the church, the Orthodox/Catholic relations are a specialty. So much is going on in this single dialogue that it is difficult to keep abreast of it. But every now and then something happens to dramatize the steady progress toward unity among Christians of the East and West. Patriarch Athanagoras visited with Pope Paul VI in Jerusalem in 1965. There they removed mutual excommunications which had been in place since 1054 when the papal legate Humbert excommunicated Michael Cerularius (who, in turn, as Patriarch of Constantinople, excommunicated the pope).

On November 30, 1979, (feast of St. Andrew, brother of St. Peter and Patron of the East), Pope John Paul II visited Istanbul. From December 3-7, 1987, Patriarch Dimitrios I, Ecumenical Patriarch of Constantinople made a return visit to the pope in Rome. On the feast of St. Andrew, Pope John Paul II sent a greeting to the Ecumenical Patriarch, inviting him to Rome and expressing his eagerness for the visit:

> This year, immediately after the feast of St. Andrew will take place your visit to Rome....The Church of Rome will receive you with profound charity. In prayer, I ask the Lord to enlighten our steps along the way which will lead us towards perfect communion so that we may celebrate his Eucharist together on the same altar. (Pope John Paul II, message for the feast of St. Andrew, *Osservatore Romano,* 7 December 1987, page 1.)

Pope John Paul II and Patriarch Dimitrios I issued a joint declaration at the end of the visit to reaffirm their desire to move ahead
in the dialogue of charity and the dialogue of faith. (The dialogue of
charity is the mutual warm relations which developed after Vatican
II between the two Apostolic Sees; the dialogue of faith is the "mixed
dialogue" between the Orthodox and the Catholic Churches which
has issued several statements on faith and practice since 1979.)

Of special importance in the joint declaration of the two
church leaders was the following statement:

> We renew before God our common pledge to promote
> by all means possible the dialogue of charity, following
> the example of Christ nourishing his church and cher-
> ishing it by his charity (cf. Eph.5:29). In this spirit, we
> reject every form of proselytizing, every attitude which
> would be or could be perceived as a lack of respect. (*Ori-
> gins* 17 [1987] p. 499)

Status of Relations

What is the status of Orthodox/Catholic relations at this time?
Obviously they are tremendously improved since pre-Vatican II
days. The Second Vatican Council clearly indicates that Rome seeks
unity with Constantinople and other Orthodox Patriarchates. It also
sets forth a new theology of the church which makes such reunion
possible without sacrificing the integrity of the autonomy of each
church. The joint statement makes this point:

> We state our joy and our satisfaction in reporting the first
> results and the positive development of the theological
> dialogue announced at the time of our meeting in Phanar
> (Istanbul) November 30, 1979. In effect they seek to
> express that which the Catholic Church and the Ortho-
> dox Church can already profess together as common faith
> about the mystery of the church and the connection
> between faith and sacraments. Each of our churches, hav-
> ing received and celebrating the same sacraments, per-
> ceives better that when unity in the faith is assured, a

certain diversity of expressions, often complementary, and of particular practices does not create obstacles to unity but enriches the life of the church and the understanding, always imperfect, of the revealed mystery. (cf. 1 Cor.13:12) (*Origins* 17 [1987] pp. 497-499)

The growing understanding of the church as mystery and as unified diversity is moving the churches steadily toward full communion. As the joint declaration affirms, there remain many obstacles yet to be overcome. Differences in theology, liturgy, and canon law require continued dialogue. However, the will to move ahead, mutual love, and respect are paving the way to unity.

Eucharistic Sharing

The ultimate goal is a sharing of the Eucharist *at the same altar.* On the Roman Catholic side, the way has been opened to a large extent by the new Code of Canon Law (Canon 844 #2, 3) which allows "eucharistic sharing" across church lines to/from the Orthodox under certain restricted conditions. The Orthodox Church is generally not in favor of eucharistic sharing at this time. However, a recent agreement between the Syrian Ancient Eastern Church and Rome (1984) permits "Communion of Hospitality" under certain conditions (not concelebration), and so does the Assyrian Ancient Eastern Church (1994). These are indications of the movements toward full communion which are under way.

The Eucharist is at the very heart of church life. Sharing the Eucharist fully is a symbol of full unity in faith and life. While we all hope and pray that such full communion may occur in *our* lifetime, we know that it will occur in *God's* good time because Jesus prayed "that all may be one" (Jn 17:21).

May

Mary and Unity

1. Mary and the Body of Christ

Mary is the *Theotokos,* the Mother of God. This affirmation of the Council of Ephesus (A.D. 431) is a statement about Jesus Christ as well as about his mother. Ephesus states that Jesus was not two persons but one, the very Son of God. If we say that Mary is his mother, we are saying that she is the mother of the Son of God.

All of Mary's privileges and titles stem from this basic fact: that she gave birth to the Christ, the Son of God. But Mary was not merely a passive instrument in the Incarnation. She played a vital and active role. The angel Gabriel was sent to ask her whether she consented to be the mother of the Savior. She said: *Let it be done to me according to your word* (Lk 1:38). She was blessed, Jesus said, because she did God's will.

This active role of Mary in salvation history is well documented in the gospel. We see her praying at Cana for the first "sign" of Jesus' ministry (Jn 2:3-6). She stands beneath the cross (Jn 19:25). She prays with the disciples in the upper room for the birth of the church (Acts 1:14), as she had prayed at Nazareth for the birth of her son. The Vatican Library has released copies of an ancient picture depicting Mary as "Mother of the Church." This portrait has Mary surrounded by the disciples in the upper room praying for the coming of the Holy Spirit.

Mary and the Bread of Life

St. Peter Julian Eymard, founder of the Congregation of the Blessed Sacrament (1811-1868), was fond of meditating on the relationship between Mary and the Eucharist. Mary gave birth to the

Bread of Life. She shared with Jesus the drama of the paschal mystery. There was an intimate bond between mother and son. Undoubtedly this bond of love and holiness was renewed and deepened as Mary shared with the disciples in the *breaking of bread*.

The Holy Spirit which descended upon the small band of disciples molded them into the church, the body of Christ. They shared, we are told by the Acts of the Apostles, in a common faith, the breaking of bread, the fellowship *(koinonia),* and prayer in common. Mary was at the center of this fellowship and shared deeply in the life of the church, as she had shared in the life of her son.

Because she shared in the communion *(koinonia)* which is the church, Mary enriched that communion by her holiness and her presence. She continues that mission or vocation today. She is mother and model of the church. If we want to know how to be Christian, we need only look at our model, Mary. She is especially a model in our relationship to the Risen Lord, present among us in the Eucharist.

Paschal Mystery/Liberation

The Eucharist is especially the paschal mystery that we celebrate and that becomes for us an instrument of salvation. The saving action of Jesus on Calvary is applied to us and our lives through the celebration of the Eucharist. Mary standing beneath the cross of Jesus is a model of our sharing in the cross of Christ. Because she shared so deeply in the cross, she shared as deeply in the glory of the Resurrection. In Mary's case, as we affirm in the dogma of the Immaculate Conception, the application of the paschal mystery to her soul was like preventive medicine. Yet she can model for us the forgiveness of sins that we daily receive in the Eucharist. She teaches us how to share the death and rising of Jesus.

Mary's contemplative soul is revealed in St. Luke's simple statement, "Mary treasured all these things, pondering them in her heart" (Lk 2:19). She prayed with the early church. She is the mother of the church today. Thus she teaches us the importance of prayer and an intimate relationship with the Risen Lord, her son. It is in our celebration of the Eucharist and our contemplation of the paschal mystery that we will find ourselves closest to Jesus and to his mother Mary.

2. Mary, the Church, and the Eucharist

In his encyclical *Redemptoris Mater,* Pope John Paul II explained that the reason for proclaiming a Marian Year was to reexamine the teachings of Vatican II about Mary and her role in salvation and the church.

The Holy Father believes there are special ecumenical gains to be had from the Marian Year, especially in terms of our relationship with the Orthodox Churches of the East. They, too, have a deep veneration and devotion to the Mother of God *(Theotokos).* This spiritual bond between East and West is important, the Holy Father states, because the church must breathe "with both lungs." Marian devotion is an example of spiritual ecumenism: making the most of what we share in common with other churches.

Mary was not a passive agent in the history of salvation. She gave birth to Jesus in her heart and mind, Augustine tells us, before she conceived him in the flesh. It was this active faith of Mary that is especially important to us as we make our pilgrim way to God and follow her example.

Mother of God, Mary is also *our* mother. She prayed with the apostles as they awaited the coming of the Holy Spirit. Mary was undoubtedly reminded of the overshadowing of the Spirit in the Incarnation, and of her awaiting the birth of Jesus, the dawn of salvation. Morning star, she announces the coming of the Son of Justice.

Mary was personally involved in the early gathering of the Christian community in the Cenacle. She prayed with the church and for the church. She continues this mission of prayerful intercession today.

At the foot of the cross, Mary received the mission of caring for all of Christ's beloved disciples. And the church, symbolized by John, received into its care and love the mother of the Redeemer of the human family. Thus, Mary became the mother of us all.

A Marian Year is, therefore, a celebration of Mary, the church, and the Eucharist. Far from presenting an obstacle to the unity of Christians, it is a help and reminder that we are all brothers and sisters in God's family. We have one mother, Mary the mother of Jesus.

3. Mary, the Eucharist, and Christian Unity

One of the difficult areas of discussion in the dialogue for Christian unity concerns the role of Mary in the church. This topic was carefully studied by the U.S. Lutheran-Roman Catholic Dialogue which published an agreed-upon statement entitled *Christ, the Mediator, Mary and the Saints.*

One of the key tenets of sixteenth-century Reformers was *solus Christus*—Christ is the sole mediator between God and humankind. The church has held this truth from the very beginning. What is at issue is the role of Mary and the saints in the church's life. As is well known, the Reformation sought to diminish this role. The reason was the superstition and abuse that sometimes existed in the Middle Ages. But, as often happens in efforts to reform, there was overreaction.

The Lutheran-Roman Catholic Dialogue emphasizes that while Jesus is the sole mediator, Mary and the saints have an important role to play in Christian piety. Martin Luther himself always preserved a tender and loving devotion to the mother of God.

This role of Mary was clearly articulated in the eighth chapter of *Lumen Gentium.* Mary is the symbol/icon of the church. She is a model for all of us in our task of imitating Christ and living his gospel.

Lumen Gentium provides a balanced and beautiful picture of what Marian devotion should be like in our lives. It provides criteria for evaluating private revelations such as at Medjugorje, Fatima, and others. Essentially private devotions have a place in the church in the measure that they reaffirm its official teaching and uphold its magisterium. Any conflict with such teaching is suspect.

Mary in Dialogue

As a result of postconciliar dialogue, the role of Mary in Catholic piety is better understood. The scriptures are clear: Mary is the mother of Jesus, who is the Son of God. She conceived him as a virgin under the power of the Holy Spirit. "Hence, the one to be born will be called holy, the Son of God" (Lk 2:35).

While Evangelical Christians may not have the same devotion as Catholic Christians, they uphold Mary's dignity. The problem is rather one of piety than of faith. In the dialogue, one of the important tasks of Catholic partners is to uphold the right of Catholic Christians to genuine devotion to Mary, while deploring the abuses of the past, and even those of the present.

Mary and the Eucharist

St. Peter Julian Eymard saw an important link between Mary and the Eucharist. He coined the title *Our Lady of the Blessed Sacrament*. A wag derided the title by asking: "Why not our Lady of the confessional?" But Pope Pius X approved the title and devotion with the words: *Ave Verum Corpus, Natum de Maria Virgine* (Hail true Body, born of the Virgin Mary). In the eighteenth century, Mozart had put these words to immortal music, heard in churches around the world ever since.

Eastern Christians underscore the role of Mary in the church and in Christian piety by continually invoking her memory in the Eucharistic Synaxis (Liturgy). "Mary, the Mother of God," St. Eymard wrote, "should not be separated from her Son in the prayer of the church."

Recalling this intimate relationship between Mary and her Son in life and in glory will be an important corrective for those who believe Marian devotion is unimportant to Christian piety. Reminding ourselves of the solid theological foundations upon which Marian devotion should rest will help us avoid the excesses and inconsistencies which otherwise make Christian unity more difficult to achieve.

Mary and Christian Unity

Mary, the Mother of Jesus, cannot be indifferent to the prayer of Jesus for Christian unity. She undoubtedly makes that prayer her own as she prays for the church. She asks for a deeper communion of all Christians in the Body of Christ. We join our prayers to hers.

June

The Eucharist: Sign and Means to Unity

1. The Eucharist and the Kingdom of God

The Gospel of Mark has Jesus begin his ministry with this proclamation: "This is the time of fulfillment. The kingdom of God is at hand. Repent, and believe the gospel" (Mk 1:15). Thus the proclamation of the kingdom of God is at the heart of the Christian message. We continue to proclaim that message as we celebrate the Eucharist.

The Kingdom of God is at Hand

One's view of the kingdom of God has an important bearing on one's view of the world. If the kingdom of God is only a spiritual kingdom realized at the end of time, then one can write off the present world as the place where God's kingdom comes.

If, on the other hand, one believes that the kingdom of God is entirely *of this world,* then the kingdom must be evaluated in terms of social progress here and now. If one believes with the church (and the gospel) that the kingdom is both here and now (Mk 1:15) and yet to come (Mk 13:3-37), then all will not be perfect in this world, but the perfect kingdom will come at the end of time. Nevertheless what we *do in this world* does make a difference for the final glory of the kingdom of God. *

The Kingdom and the Church

At various times the church itself was seen as the kingdom of God. There are reasons for thinking in this way. The Gospel of

Matthew would support the view that various sayings of Jesus speak of the church of the future and the kingdom of God (Mt 14-18).

When church and state were one it was easy to think that the kingdom was one with the church. This view easily gave birth to the idea that only the *true* church, that is, the Church of Rome, was the kingdom, and other churches were outside it. Vatican II, however, teaches that the Body of Christ, the church and the kingdom embrace all of the baptized, whether in our church or in other Christian communions.

Christ, the King of Peace

The preface from the liturgy of the Feast of Christ the King speaks of a kingdom of "justice, love and peace." That kingdom is something which *begins* to be realized *in this world* as well as in the next. Its *full* realization awaits the return of the Lord Jesus in glory, but signs of its reality appear in the lives of Christians and other believers as well as in what they do for others.

The Kingdom in This World

Pierre Teilhard de Chardin, Jesuit priest, mystic, and scientist, wrote in glowing terms of his hope for the world. He believed that the world was moving inexorably toward *point omega,* at which time Jesus would come again in glory. While he acknowledged the problem of sin ("human drag") and the reality of human freedom (one can choose to do wrong rather than right), he believed that God wills a continuing development of the world and humankind. Thus he saw a relationship between human efforts for the improvement of science and technology, and for the development of the human spirit through education and the arts. Spiritual growth is an important dimension of his world view.

The Kingdom and the Eucharist

The Eucharist is a proclamation of the gospel, and of the kingdom of God. "Christ has died, Christ is risen, Christ will come again!"

remains the reason for Christian hope as we celebrate the breaking of bread and the sharing of the cup. Christ will come again in glory with salvation for his people. The salvation of Christ is shared in each Eucharist.

This is a hope that we all share. As we recall the blessings and achievements of the year, we give thanks to God that his kingdom has come to a greater extent in our world. We live in grace and the hope for the final victory at the end of time. Meanwhile, we ask God's help and the gift of his Spirit so that we may be instruments of peace and justice to build God's kingdom in faith and love.

2. The Eucharist and the Forgiveness of Sins

A casual look at the newspapers or the television news — indeed a glance at our neighborhood or a personal examination of conscience—will readily convince us of the reality of sin. The scriptures are filled with the idea that God's people is a sinful people. The gospels are more hopeful. They tell us that God's sinful people were redeemed in the blood of Christ. And yet sin remains a fact of life.

At times we seem overwhelmed by the extent of sin in our world. The marginalization of entire peoples and cultures seems beyond our capability of restoring human rights and human dignity. The struggle for peace is continuous.

And yet the Eucharist directly answers our need for peace, justice and goodness. This memorial *(anamnesis)* or remembrance of the fact/event of the saving sacrifice of Jesus, tells us that we share in the redemption of Jesus Christ each time the bread is broken and the cup poured out "for the forgiveness of sins." Jesus Christ died that the world might have life and be freed from sin.

While liberation theologians stress the social aspects of this teaching, the liturgy stresses the communal and personal dimensions. In other words, we are challenged by the redeeming Lord to be instruments of salvation in our world.

The Forgiveness of Sins

We usually think of the sacrament of reconciliation as the sacrament for the forgiveness of sins. But the Eucharist is also a sacrament of forgiveness. This may seem a bit confusing, but let me try to explain.

The Council of Trent indicated that forgiveness comes from true contrition. Contrition is normally related to the sacrament of reconciliation. However, other sacraments, especially the Eucharist, can and do develop contrition and the dispositions that are required for forgiveness.

Forgiveness of sins begins at baptism (surely the outstanding sacrament of forgiveness) and continues throughout life, until the final reconciliation with the Lord in viaticum.

The Synod of Bishops on the sacrament of reconciliation (1986) stressed the need to see in the sacrament of reconciliation more than a magical formula for disposing of one's "dirty laundry." Reconciliation/forgiveness is always related to contrition and one's desire to change or improve one's life (conversion).

The Eucharist and Forgiveness

The Eucharist is given to us "for the remission of sins which we daily commit." The words of institution, in particular over the cup, emphasize that the blood of Christ is/was "poured out for the remission of sins."

The practical importance of this teaching can be seen from a realization of how little a sense of sin exists in our world. Ethical and moral standards are rarely the subject of education, whether in the home or the school. What is legal or what one can "get away with" is often the only concern in public or private life.

The new rites of reconciliation help us to realize that sin has a personal and communal dimension. We not only offend God by sin, we also harm the Body of Christ. Sin is a sickness affecting the whole body. Hence the importance of recognizing it, and seeking to cure it in all its dimensions. In this respect the Eucharist and our common acknowledgment that we need forgiveness can be helpful.

Conclusion

We need to see more clearly that the Eucharist is the center of our Christian life. The Eucharist reminds us that we have been baptized in Christ; we share his cross and his mission. As he gave his life so that the world might be less sinful and more holy, so we must live our lives in greater holiness. Because the Eucharist is given "for the forgiveness of sins," there is hope for us and our sinful world.

3. The Eucharist: A Call to Solidarity

One of the major contributions of John Paul II to the improvement of social conditions is his encyclical *Sollicitudo Rei Socialis* (On Social Concern). Its central theme is that true human development cannot be limited to economic and political considerations:

> When individuals and communities do not see a rigorous respect for the moral, cultural and spiritual requirements, based on the dignity of the person and on the proper identity of each community, beginning with the family and religious societies, then all the rest—availability of goods, abundance of technical resources applied to daily life, a certain level of material well-being—will prove unsatisfying and in the end contemptible. (SRS #33)

In another section of this encyclical the pope develops the relationship between the "kingdom of God" and concern about human development. He emphasizes that the ultimate goal will be reached only when Jesus comes again in glory to establish permanently his eternal kingdom. Until then we are engaged in efforts to make our world a reflection of that kingdom. Every success will contribute to the kingdom, and no effort will be lost.

In this context Pope John Paul develops the idea that the Eucharist is a call to solidarity in our efforts to reach the kingdom of God. It is a reflection of God's kingdom in its final reality.

> All of us who take part in the Eucharist are called to discover, through this sacrament, the profound *meaning* of

our actions in the world in favor of development and peace; and to receive from it the strength to commit ourselves ever more generously, following the example of Christ, who in this sacrament lays down his life for his friends (cf. Jn 15:13). Our personal commitment, like Christ's and in union with his, will not be in vain but certainly fruitful. (SRS #48)

The Eucharist makes us one with Christ. This unity with our Lord gives us communion *(koinonia)* with the Father, Son and Spirit. Our communion is also with all other Christians in Christ. This communion, begun in baptism, is deepened in the Eucharist. We are challenged by the Eucharist to work together for the "kingdom of God," for the human rights and development of all persons.

This strong message of the encyclical, *On Social Concern,* is one we need to take to heart. We must find in the Eucharist the motive and the strength we need for pastoral efforts on behalf of the people of God, the church and the human family.

We think too often of the sacraments in individualistic terms: God and I. Similarly we think of the church as a society to be protected from heresy and intruders. Our challenge is to see the church as an instrument of salvation for the world (as Christ was), and the sacraments as the means to this salvation. We are sanctified by the sacraments (encounters with Christ) so that we might *transform* the world by our Christian concern and ministry.

Ecumenical Dimensions

This insight into the nature of the church and the Eucharist will help us to understand we are challenged and compelled to solidarity with other Christians in our efforts to renew the world in which we live. No church is large enough or strong enough to go it alone. The task is too great, the obstacles too numerous for us to build the kingdom of God by our isolated efforts. Pope John Paul emphasizes that all Christians and all people of faith must work together to achieve the goals of the gospel in the area of social concern.

Shelter for the homeless, food for the hungry, clothing for the naked, help for the poor, jobs for the unemployed, assistance to the elderly, education and guidance for the young, do not require Catholic membership. But, they demand solidarity in social concern. The Eucharist presents this challenge to us and assures us of the strength of Christ in its pursuit.

4. The Eucharist: Christ's Sacrifice and Ours

The Eucharist is the paschal mystery, Christ's sacrifice and our own. The sacrificial nature of the Eucharist is clearly affirmed in the gospels. However, the explanation of *how* the Eucharist is a sacrifice has been a matter of study and debate for centuries.

This debate became more sharply polemical at the time of the Reformation. The Council of Trent preserved the notion and belief that the Eucharist is a sacrifice. It appealed to the fathers of the church and especially to the medieval theologians to explain this concept.

A century ago the sacrificial nature of the Eucharist was seen either in its nature as an *offering,* or in its symbolic *immolation.* The latter concept was current even as the church entered the Second Vatican Council. However at that time it was already seen as deficient. The idea of sacrifice as self-offering began to prevail.

A brief reflection like this can only recall the theological debate that surrounds this question. More profitably it can touch upon the major areas of agreement, especially in the light of recent bilateral and multilateral dialogue.

Christ's Sacrifice

The Letter to the Hebrews states clearly that Christ offered his sacrifice *once for all.* On Calvary Christ redeemed us all. If the Eucharist is a sacrifice, it can only be in some sense and some way *his* sacrifice. And this is what the church teaches: that the *same* sacrifice is offered "now in an unbloody manner" as once it was offered in its bloody reality.

The best way to explain how the Eucharist is the sacrifice of Christ is to say that *we share* in his sacrifice. There is an *eternal dimension* to his sacrifice which remains. We, in time, reach into, so to speak, that eternal dimension and apply it to time. (Christ is the one who applies his sacrifice to us "for the remission of sins.")

The Eucharist is the sacrifice of the church because it is the offering of Christ, the head of the church. We, as members of the Mystical Body of Christ, offer the Eucharist *with Christ and in Christ.* And this sacrifice is pleasing to the Father because it is the self-offering of Jesus and the members of his Body. Indeed, as St. Augustine points out, we become the Body of Christ through the Eucharist that we offer.

Our Sacrifice

Much of the controversy surrounding the Eucharist as sacrifice originated from the desire for holiness in the church. Many were quite disgusted with the nominalism of the time. Nominalism was more than a philosophy; it colored the attitude of many Christians. The mere name *Christian* was not enough for Catholic and Protestant reformers. They wanted Christians who were truly followers of Christ.

Applying this point of view to the Eucharist (as did the Council of Trent to a large extent), it is not enough that we be *nominally* involved in the Eucharist. It must become *our* sacrifice. How can this be done?

Theologians say today that the core of the Eucharist as sacrifice is self-offering. What made the sacrifice of Jesus Christ pleasing to the Father was not the blood and gore of Calvary. It was the self-offering of Jesus. Jesus offered himself to the Father at the Last Supper, at Gethsemane in the Agony in the Garden, from the first moment of his existence (Heb 10:45) and throughout his life. But the high point of his self-offering was when he loved the Father and us "to the end" and gave his life "for us and our salvation."

As Jesus was one who came "not to be served, but to serve" (Mk 10:45), so we are called to celebrate in the Eucharist our service and self-sacrifice for others.

5. The Church: A Eucharistic Communion

At the present time it is very easy for us to think of the church as an institution—as a world-wide organization with its offices at the Vatican and its authority in the pope. It is more difficult for us to think of the church as a local community—a communion or fellowship of believers centered around the local bishop. However, the ancient paradigm of the church is much more the latter than the former. While the primacy of the pope has been recognized since the beginning, the church was seen much more as the local community joining its bishop in the celebration of the Eucharist.

This is why such a great variety of rites and languages and liturgical practices grew up in the first centuries of the church. Centralization of liturgical practice came more slowly. While there were advantages to the codification of the liturgy (the twelfth century was characterized by such a striving for uniformity), still something was lost—notably the understanding of the church as a local community celebrating the Eucharist.

In his book *Dare to Believe,* Cardinal Lustiger states that the church is never more itself than when it is celebrating the Eucharist. In the Eucharist the church finds its identity as a community of faith. The Eucharist celebrates the faith of the church and deepens it. It celebrates the hope of the church and strengthens it. It celebrates the love of the church and enlivens it. Once the church has celebrated the Eucharist it is ready to renew its commitment to its mission, spreading the good news of Christ as Savior of the world and establishing his kingdom of peace and justice.

The Church and Mission

If the church is a eucharistic community, its mission is related to the Eucharist. Its task is "to unite into one the divided children of God" (Jn 11:52). The unity of the church is an essential part of its mission. The Eucharist is the grace and means to achieve its task.

But the church does not exist for itself. It exists for the world. In this it imitates its founder who came not to be served but to serve and lay down his life for the ransom of the many (Mk 26:26). Reaching out to others in a desire for communion is the mission of every Christian.

Jesus prayed "that all may be one...so that the world may believe that you sent me" (Jn 17:21). The evangelization of the world requires the unity of Christians. And so ecumenism is not peripheral to the church's mission. It is vital to it. And the carrying out of this task is both symbolized and realized by the Eucharist and the unity it produces.

The Eucharist and the Church

We think it is important to recall that the church is *essentially* a euchartistic community. As we celebrate the Eucharist we build the church and fulfill its mission.

6. Christian Unity and the Eucharist

We prepare for the third millennium. Important areas of the Christian life have been targeted for the church's renewal: family life, spiritual and liturgical renewal, leadership development, shared ministry, integral education, justice, evangelization, communication and stewardship.

The Eucharist "is the summit toward which the activity of the church is directed; it is also the fount from which all her power flows" (SC #10). From the Eucharist flows the grace needed for the Christian life. The Eucharist celebrates our achievements to the glory of God. "For the goal of apostolic endeavor is that all who are made sons of God by faith and baptism should come together to praise God in the midst of his church, to take part in the Sacrifice and to eat the Lord's Supper" (ibid.).

Underlying all our pastoral efforts should be a realization that the unity of the church is fundamental. The unity of all Catholics and the unity of all Christians is the most important goal of the church today. Just as the second millennium saw the breakdown of Christian unity, so the third millennium must see its restoration. This is the stated goal of the present Holy Father, Pope John Paul II, reflecting the Second Vatican Council.

It isn't easy to realize that working for Christian unity is not something one does *after* everything else. It must be seen as *part and parcel* of all that we do as Christians. This is particularly true of the Eucharist. We cannot celebrate the Eucharist without a keen sense of the division which exists among all who are baptized in Christ. East and West, Protestant and Catholic, Evangelical and Pentecostal are divided by centuries of hostility.

While theological bridges continue to be built over the chasm of separation, the churches are far from reconciled. For complete reconciliation more than theology or ecclesiastical agreements are needed. Christians everywhere must come to realize the scandal of their division and the call for continued prayer and effort "that all may be one...so that the world will believe" (Jn 17:21).

Before the churches can be reunited, Christians must rediscover their own unity in Christ Jesus. Once they have discovered this unity they will find compelling reasons for working together in projects of all kinds for the betterment of the human family. As long as Christians are involved with family feuds inherited from the past, they are unable to get on with the tremendous task that the world and the Lord call them to perform.

This task includes improving family life, developing spiritual and liturgical practice, leadership development, shared ministry, integral education. It especially involves work for justice and peace, evangelization (spreading the good news of salvation in Jesus Christ), communication among Christians and all people of good will, and a sense of stewardship (the sharing of God-given gifts of time, talent and money).

We should realize that the Eucharist must deepen our unity as Catholics and our unity with all other Christians. The heart of this unity is our communion *(koinonia)* with our savior, Jesus Christ. Through the eucharistic celebration, our reception of the Bread of Life and our eucharistic contemplation, we will drawer closer to him and to each other.

7. The Eucharist: Praise and Thanksgiving to the Father

Many Christians are not sufficiently conscious of the fact that their faith and worship is essentially trinitarian; that is, orientated toward God the Father in the Son and Spirit. They wonder how they should pray. Jesus clearly indicated that we should pray to the Father ("When you pray, say 'Our Father...'" Mt. 6:9ff). Not only our prayer, but also our lives should be so directed.

In a major statement of Christian unity, The World Council of Churches in its Faith and Order Commission's *Baptism, Eucharist, and Ministry* (BEM) [Geneva, 1982], makes the point in these words:

> The Eucharist, which always includes both word and sacrament, is a proclamation and a celebration of the work of God. It is the great thanksgiving to the Father for everything accomplished in creation, redemption, and sanctification, for everything accomplished by God now in the church church and in the world in spite of the sins of human beings, for everything that God will accomplish in bringing the Kingdom to fulfillment. Thus the Eucharist is the benediction (berakah) by which the Church expresses its thankfulness for all God's benefits. (Euch. #3)

This orientation is a very hopeful one. It stresses that all is in God's hands and unfolds according to his plan. We are not ships tossing in a sea. Life is a gift, and so is grace. At the Eucharist we count our blessings and give thanks for them.

Through the Eucharist, we acknowledge that we are not in a perfect world. Man's sinfulness and unwillingness to seek God's will and fulfill it leads to untold miseries for many human beings. The Eucharist asks forgiveness for such sinfulness. It also proclaims the hope that God's grace will overcome human sin and shortcomings.

In this perception of reality, all is gift. The Eucharist is our expression of thanks in Christ and through him:

> The Eucharist is the great sacrifice of praise by which the church speaks on behalf of the whole of creation. For the world which God has reconciled is present at every Eucharist: in the bread and wine, in the persons of the faithful, and in the prayers they offer for themselves and for all people. Christ united the faithful with Himself and includes their prayers within His own intercession so that the faithful are transfigured and their prayers accepted. This sacrifice of praise is possible only through Christ, with Him and in Him. The bread and wine, fruits of the earth and of human labor, are presented to the Father in faith and thanksgiving. The Eucharist thus signifies what the world is to become: an offering and hymn of praise to the Creator, a universal communion in the body of Christ, a kingdom of justice, love, and peace in the Holy Spirit. (Euch. #4)

We believe—and the *Baptism, Eucharist, and Ministry* (BEM) document describes it in another section (see Euch. #15)—that the bread and wine are transformed into the Body and Blood of Christ. What the document emphasizes here is that all of creation is taken up in the Sacrifice of Christ and transformed into a hymn of praise.

The Eucharist, then, is a challenge to all of us to transform creation, the world around us, as we are transfigured by Christ. Our worship transforms our life. Our life renews the world.

The Roman Catholic Church is a member of the Faith and Order Commission of the World Council of Churches. It is a part of the convergence which the BEM document expresses. The statement is both a foundation for future unity in the church, and a means for transforming Christians so that such unity is possible. By revitalizing our faith in the Eucharist and our celebration of it, BEM contributes to our Christian living and our hope for the future of the church.

8. Eucharist: Memorial and Communion

The Anglican-Roman Catholic dialogue has produced *substantial agreement* on doctrinal teaching concerning the Eucharist. This is an important step toward the unity of the two churches.

> An important stage in progress toward organic unity is a substantial consensus on the purpose and meaning of the Eucharist. Our intention has been to seek a deeper understanding of the reality of the Eucharist which is consonant with biblical teaching and with the tradition of our common inheritance, and to express in this document the consensus we have reached. (*Final Report*/Euch. #1)

The deeper understanding which the *Final Report* speaks of focuses on the Eucharist as memorial (*anamnesis*) and communion (*koinonia*). I would like to say a word about them here.

Memorial

According to the *Final Report,* the Eucharist is a memorial of the Passover Mystery/Event which Jesus experienced at the end of his life. For some the Eucharist is seen as an exact replica of the event in all its details. Somehow the Mass is a repetition of what happened then. How this occurs they find difficult to explain. While this may be a popular view for some Christians, it is *not* "consonant with biblical teaching and with the tradition of our common inheritance." The *Final Report* explains:

Christ's redeeming death and resurrection took place
once and for all in history. Christ's death on the cross,
the culmination of his whole life of obedience, was the
one, perfect, and sufficient sacrifice for the sins of the
world. There can be no repetition of, or addition to, what
was then accomplished once for all by Christ. Any
attempt to express a nexus between the sacrifice of
Christ and the eucharist must not obscure this fundamental fact of Christian faith. (*Final Report*/Euch. #5)

On the other hand the notion of *memorial* is deeply rooted in
biblical tradition and does shed much light on the nature of the
eucharistic sacrifice.

The notion of memorial as understood in the passover celebration at the time of Christ—i.e. the making effective in
the present of an event in the past—has opened the way to a
clearer understanding of the relationship between Christ's
sacrifice and the eucharist. (*Final Report*/Euch. #5)

The statement continues and says the Eucharist is "no mere calling
to mind of a past event or of its significance, but the church's effec-
tual proclamation of God's mighty acts" (*Final Report*/Euch. #5).

Communion

The purpose of the Eucharist is "to transmit the life of the crucified and risen Christ to His body, the church, so that its members
may be more fully united with Christ and with one another" (*Final
Report*/Euch. #6). Communion with the Lord through the Eucharist
presupposes both the real presence of Christ "effectually signified
by the bread and wine which, in this mystery, become His body and
blood" (*Final Report*/Euch. #6) and the faith of the receiver who wel-
comes the Lord *in faith* (see *Final Report*/Euch.-Elucidation #7).

As the document stresses, it is not enough for the sacrament to
be real that Jesus be present *for* the recipient. He must also be present *with* the receiver.

The sacramental body and blood of the Savior are present as an offering to the believer awaiting His welcome. When this offering is met by faith, a life-giving encounter results. Through faith Christ's presence—which does not depend on the individual's faith in order to be the Lord's real gift of Himself to His Church—becomes no longer just a presence FOR the believer, but also a presence WITH him. Thus, in considering the mystery of the eucharistic presence, we must recognize both the sacramental sign of Christ's presence and the personal relationship between Christ and the faithful which arises from that presence. (*Final Report*/Euch. #8)

These two emphases of memorial and communion are important to Anglican and Roman Catholic understanding of the Eucharist. Substantial agreement on this subject gives hope for unity and reconciliation of the churches.

As Pope John Paul II wrote to Archbishop Runcie of Canterbury, Rome's position on Anglican Orders and the problem of women's ordination are obstacles to unity. "They must be overcome. We celebrate the Eucharist in divided Churches, yet there is hope that the Lord who presents Himself to each believer will unite us to himself and to each other in growing unity."

9. Is Eucharistic Hospitality Permissible?

This question cannot be answered simply yes or no. The question raises many issues that need to be considered as one tries to answer the question.

For Roman Catholics the canonical answer is found in the 1983 Code of Canon Law (Can #844), which not only indicates an affirmative answer, but states the times and places and circumstances when Catholics may receive the Eucharist in another church and when others may receive in a Catholic church.

In general, the canon states, people should receive in their own churches. This is because the Eucharist is a sign of union with Christ, but it is also a sign of communion in faith. Thus there is an *ecclesial* element in the reception of the Eucharist. (Since Eastern Catholics are in *full communion* with Rome, hospitality is always permitted between Eastern and Western Catholics; for example, Maronites, Ruthenians, Melkites, etc.)

The canon further indicates that for spiritual benefit Catholics may receive in Orthodox churches and Orthodox may receive in Catholic churches because both churches are considered to be in almost full communion by Rome. The problem with this solution is that the Orthodox Church (except for the Oriental Orthodox of Syria) generally does not accept Roman Catholic ecclesiology—it has a different understanding of church.

Further the canon indicates that Catholics may receive for the same reasons from other churches that are in *the same condition* as the Orthodox as far as Roman recognition of the sacrament of

Orders (such as the Old Catholics of Utrecht, the Polish National Church, and the like).

When it comes to Protestant Churches of the Reformation (Anglicans, Lutherans, Reformed, etc.) there is a radical difference. Their members may receive from Catholic ministers (priests, deacons, eucharistic ministers) under certain circumstances, but Roman Catholics may not receive from their ordained ministers, according to canon 844, #4.

On the other hand, the rule for the Anglican Communion (including the Episcopal church in the U.S.A.) invites all baptized Christians to receive the Eucharist. Lutherans and Episcopalians may receive in each other's church under the provisions of "Interim Eucharistic Sharing," established by joint agreement in 1982.

Finally it should be noted that eucharistic hospitality would not be welcomed by some Protestant churches, while others might practice open communion, allowing all baptized Christians to receive in their church.

Theological Considerations

As one can see by simply looking at canonical provisions, the matter is not simple or self-evident.

In 1993 The World Council of Churches held its Faith and Order Conference in Santiago, Spain. One of the provisions of a draft document is for further eucharistic sharing. The document points out that some churches already have such provisions (such as the Episcopal/Lutheran agreement). Others have extended a call for such sharing, but have not been favorably received, such as the Roman Catholic invitation to Orthodox Churches.

Why is eucharistic hospitality so important to the ecumenical movement? First of all because it is the goal of the ecumenical movement to have one eucharistic fellowship. The sign of the church is the Eucharist. If the church is one, the sign of that unity will be (it is not yet) a shared Eucharist.

The Roman Catholic objection to shared Eucharist is that there is insufficient sharing of faith at this time. While dialogue is moving the Christian churches together, there still remain substantial disagreements in major areas of church teaching. Until these disagreements are resolved, Rome feels intercommunion would be premature.

It is important to note that Rome is talking about *intercommunion,* not about eucharistic sharing. Ecumenists point out the difference: intercommunion is a permanent arrangement that follows recognition of the existence of *full communion* and allows persons from one church to receive in another at will. It also supposes mutual recognition of ministries (ordinations).

Eucharistic hospitality is an occasional reception of the Eucharist in a church other than one's own. This could be done for spiritual motives or because one is in critical need. The latter would occur if a person were in serious illness and without a minister of one's own.

Conclusion

In this time of transition and development, it is important that we all try to understand the reasons for the church's legislation. It is equally important to know that this is not a permanent state of things. We continue to move forward to a church united and sharing together the Bread of Life.

The 1993 Directory for the Application of Principles and Norms on Ecumenism explains the breadth of eucharistic sharing possibilities under present canonical legislation.

July

Marriage and Christian Unity

1. Communion in the Domestic Church

There is an important convergence of images and ideas around communion, the church and the family. St. Paul, in his letter to the Ephesians, reminds Christians that there is a great mystery symbolized by the love of husband and wife, and that is the love of Christ for his church (Eph 5:32).

Very often married couples feel this image of Christ and his church is too lofty an ideal for them to find inspiration in it for their daily lives. And yet this is precisely what they are called to do by the sacrament of matrimony. The Christian ideal for marriage and the family is impossible without the grace of God. But with that grace the Christian life becomes enfleshed in the love that two people have for each other, and is incarnated in the children who are given life because of that love.

The encyclical of John Paul II's *Familiaris Consortio* (On the Family), is a neglected source of inspiration in our time. Yet it is filled with great wisdom and the great tradition on marriage that should be meditated on and can provide inspiration for Christian families.

> The Holy Spirit, who is poured forth in the celebration of the sacraments, is the living source and inexhaustible sustenance of the supernatural communion that gathers believers and links them with Christ and with each other in the unity of the church of God. The Christian family constitutes a specific revelation and realization of the ecclesial communion, and for this reason too it can and should be called **"the domestic church."** (Fam. Consort. #21)

Domestic Church

The term *domestic church* originated with the practice of the early Christians gathering in homes for the celebration of the Eucharist. At a time when Jewish practice still influenced Christians a great deal, religious meals in the family setting were still the norm. During the persecutions, it was a safe place.

Gradually the church became institutionalized, and with Constantine's Edict of Milan there was no longer a need for the church to worship in hiding. From that moment on churches took the shape of the basilica (the royal banquet rooms) and the days of the domestic church as the normal setting for the Eucharist were over.

The church cannot go back to those days, though post-Vatican II permission to celebrate home masses is deeply appreciated in the wake of the Council's liturgical renewal. Our point here is not liturgical, but theological. In recent years, the concept of the family as the domestic church has gained acceptance. It implies that the church is the "family of families" and that the church is alive in the family.

The concept of domestic church is even richer than this simple reality. It is intimately tied to the concept of the church as communion. If the paradigm for the church is the trinity of persons in God, this same paradigm is verified in the domestic church, the family. Paul talks about the love of Christ for the church as "the great mystery." It is the incarnation of God's love for his people. And the love of husband and wife is a sharing in the love of Christ for his church.

The love of parents for children is also understood in the love of God for his children whom we are. Thus love (communion) is the "heart" of the family, the church—and ultimately, God—for "God is love" (1 Jn 4:16).

Renewing the Family

A constant refrain is that our culture, especially by its individualism and self-centeredness, has contributed greatly to the breakdown of the family, and ultimately of society. All are aware of developing new models and images for the restoration of the family. (An article in *Christian Century* by Robert Bellah and Christopher

Freeman Adams points to the family as one of the important institutions needing renewal for "the good city.")

I suggest that John Paul II's image of the family as the domestic church renewed by deeper communion with God in Christ is a good place to begin the renewal of the family, the domestic church, and the renewal of the church, the family of families.

Interchurch Families

I find this idea of communion in the domestic church particularly compelling in the discussion of interchurch families. Just as the communion of the church is broken by the centuries of division in the church—to the scandal of the world—so the restoration of communion will rebuild the unity of the Body of Christ which is the church. The church and the family should mirror the love of God in the trinity of persons: Father, Son and Spirit. The Son was sent to mankind by the Father "to reconcile everything in Christ." All Christians must be involved in this saving work of reconciliation (2 Cor 5:18-21). And this is at the heart of the ecumenical movement.

Interchurch families experience the agony and the ecstasy of the ecumenical dilemma. We are called to be one, and yet we are separated by the divisions that have marred the church down through the centuries. These divisions today are within the church as well as among the churches—hence the pressing need to deepen the communion which must exist in the domestic church and in the church universal.

2. Interchurch Families: Celebrating Baptism

As I have often indicated, interchurch families are at the cutting edge of the ecumenical question. This is not to say that ideally Catholics should not marry persons who are Catholic. Rather, when people choose to do otherwise, they personally experience the pain, frustration and problems that the church experiences because of the historic divisions which wound her and tear the seamless garment of Christ.

I received a telephone call from the diocese of Albany, New York, on the subject of baptism in interchurch families. The person who called indicated that the Anglican-Roman Catholic Dialogue there found it a "sticky" issue and wanted some help.

In a short reflection like this, it is impossible to treat this subject adequately, but I thought it might be useful to recall some general principles that can easily be forgotten when this subject is discussed, or when clergy and interchurch families are involved.

The Church is a Communion

One important principle rediscovered at the Second Vatican Council is that the church is a communion. All those who are baptized and believe in Jesus Christ as Son of God and Savior are part of that communion of faith.

One often hears Catholics speak of other Christians as belonging "to another faith" or another "religion." Such terms do not accurately describe the reality or what the church has understood and proclaimed in Vatican II. Similarly some Protestants describe themselves as "Christians" but sometimes fail to realize that Catholics are Christians too.

In the words of Vatican II, the Catholic Church believes it is in various levels of communion with other Christians. Eastern Rite Catholics and Roman Catholics are "in full communion." The Orthodox Churches are described by the Council as in "almost full communion." This terminology is used in all official documents of the church, including agreed statements produced through the Orthodox-Catholic Dialogue. (Eastern Rite Catholics accept the primacy of the pope, the Orthodox do not. There are other differences between Rome and Constantinople, as is clear from the Orthodox-Catholic Dialogue.)

Anglicans, Lutherans, and Protestants are described in the words of Vatican II as being "in **real** though imperfect communion." It is important to note that all other Christians are *in communion* with the church, though that communion is not perfect. It needs to be improved by dialogue and by changes. (The church acknowledges that reform and change are required within the Catholic Church as well.)

Baptism

There was a time when baptisms outside the community of faith were questioned. Heretics were thought to be incapable of validly baptizing other Christians. This was the view of St. Cyprian and continues to be held in the Orthodox church today. St. Augustine, however, defended the idea that it is Christ who baptizes and gives grace in the sacraments. Therefore the validity of sacraments does not depend upon the worthiness of the minister. Augustine's view prevailed in the Western church.

Similarly the baptisms performed in emergency situations by the laity were questioned. But one thousand years ago the church decided that such baptisms were indeed valid and not to be repeated. All that is required for valid baptism is that the person who baptizes intends to do what Christ and the church intend. The

validity of baptisms performed in other Christian churches, therefore, must also be valid.

Where to Baptize

Where the question becomes "sticky," in the words of my
interlocutor, is when a couple begins to put together a baptismal cer-
emony for an interchurch family. Who should be the minister?
Where should the baptism be performed? What rite should be followed? Who should be the sponsors?

While there is an official Roman Catholic position on these
questions described in Canon Law, there are many other considerations, especially ecumenical, which may not be so neatly covered.
For example, which of the parents goes to church? Where will the
children worship? Who will see to it that the children are more than
nominally attached to a given church?

Other considerations: sponsors represent not the parents or
the family, but the community of faith to which they belong. They
should consequently belong to the church in which the children are
baptized.

As in interchurch marriages, it is appropriate that the rite of
baptism be that of the place—if the parish church is Catholic, the rite
should be Catholic; if it is Protestant, the rite should be Protestant,
etc. It is important to note that the Orthodox Church does not officially recognize sacraments performed by other Christian churches.
Also the Catholic Church requires Catholic parents to have their
children baptized as Catholics.

A simple rule of thumb could be: the procedure used for interchurch weddings should be applied to interchurch baptisms. The
help of the parish priest should be sought as well. Such baptisms
afford another opportunity to mend ecumenical relations and promote Christian unity.

3. Interchurch Families: Where in the Church?

Pope John Paul II has stated that interchurch couples are on the "cutting edge" of the ecumenical question. They are living out daily the struggle that the church endures to be one. The love that binds them together is a symbol of the love that eventually must conquer the divisions of Christianity as a whole.

Vatican II states that members of other Christian churches are "in a real though imperfect communion" with the church of Rome. This communion is a union in faith, hope and love with Jesus Christ and the Trinity symbolized by baptism. Paul's statement about "One Lord, one faith, one baptism" (Eph 4:6) expresses this communion shared by all Christians.

Pope John Paul II in *Familiaris Consortio* states that the sacrament of marriage unites the non-Catholic spouse to the Catholic partner *and to the Catholic Church* in a special way.

While the communion spoken of in Vatican II and the special relationship mentioned by Pope John Paul II has not found its way into the Code of Canon Law, it does begin to explain why Pope Paul VI in *Matrimonia Mixta* (1970) called for special pastoral care and ministry to interchurch families.

Education of Children

One of the special concerns of the church and of parents in interchurch families is the education of children. Catholic partners sign promises before obtaining a dispensation to marry a non-Catholic partner. These promises indicate that the Catholic party will do everything possible to see that the children receive training in the Catholic faith.

Those involved in ecumenical ministry emphasize that the obligation to educate children religiously is incumbent upon *both parents*. This is the very nature of things. Education of children begins at birth and continues throughout life. One cannot *postpone* religious education any more than one can postpone teaching behavior, attitude and other facts of life. As soon as a child can learn to read and write (and even before) there is much education that can be imparted.

Parents in interchurch families should be encouraged to work at Christian education *together*. Indeed at the elementary level Christian education in every church is very similar: teaching about the Bible, the gospels, goodness and truth, self-sacrifice and service.

What makes churches different is something that even adults have a hard time understanding. Moreover the work of theologians today is to dialogue and thus raise the many teachings that the churches have in common and indicate the very few things that are *church-dividing*.

Prayer and Worship

Another important area of life for interchurch couples is that of prayer and worship. While deciding which church to attend may be a more difficult question, prayer in the home is always possible. Christians share the Bible together (Old and New Testaments), believe in the necessity and usefulness of prayer, possess many common traditions, values and practices.

Rather than emphasize those things that are distinctly Catholic, it would be useful to strengthen interchurch family life and spiritual development to make the most of those elements couples have in common. As for liturgical worship, these can be shared together alternately or (if the non-Catholic partner feels comfortable in doing so) by worshiping together at the Catholic parish.

Modern movements (ecumenical, liturgical, biblical, and charismatic) have brought about a marvelous similarity between

Catholic and non-Catholic worship. These common elements need to be stressed in interchurch families.

Eucharist

While sharing the Eucharist is the ultimate goal of the church's search for unity, interchurch families have much to suffer from existing rules about eucharistic communion. Nevertheless there are times and circumstances when the unity achieved and the unity desired by the church allow for *eucharistic sharing.* The bishop indicates when such sharing is appropriate and allowed. Meanwhile we pray together that the progress in unity among all Christians may soon make it possible for interchurch families to receive the Eucharist together on a regular basis.

4. Interchurch Marriage

Because of the present ecumenical climate, or perhaps in spite of it, we are experiencing more interchurch marriages than ever before. Part of the reason is simply the mobility of people and the plurality of cultures and religious traditions which populate our planet.

There was a time when interchurch marriages were rare, and people who entered them were made to feel very guilty about having done so. In the Catholic Church, such marriages were celebrated in the rectory, and only the witnesses were allowed to attend. Church law required dispensations and promises from both parties about the Catholic upbringing of the children. Some of this legislation remains. So does some of the opposition to interchurch marriages.

We must admit candidly that interchurch marriages, and even more, interreligious ones, do present problems, especially in today's world with Christendom divided. However the atmosphere is changing considerably in the light of a growing sense of the unity of the church and the mounting imperative for Christians to work together.

For many centuries the problems of interchurch marriages were laid at the doorstep of the couple itself. "They should marry their own kind," was frequently on the lips of family and friends. Today the churches admit that the church itself is at fault because of its divisions.

Shortly after Vatican II with its momentous steps toward unity, Paul VI signed a document called *Matrimonia Mixta* (1970). It was published after much study by various departments of the Vatican in order to answer the needs of interchurch and interreligious couples. One of the most important changes that was introduced was the discontinuance of signed promises by the non-Catholic person. Only the Catholic party was required to sign promises (obviously without jeopardizing the marriage itself) to see that the children were baptized and raised as Catholics.

Further, the document requested that for mixed marriages the priest and minister should get together to appropriately prepare the couple and assist them in their married life. The tenor of the document clearly indicates that a greater openness toward such couples is needed. This openness is reflected in the encyclical of Pope John Paul II, *Familiaris Consortio,* and the statements he makes concerning mixed marriages.

A Dilemma

Interchurch couples today need understanding and sympathy from people in every Christian church. They are, as Pope John Paul II says, "on the cutting edge" of the ecumenical problem. They love each other, but are in churches that are divided. Indeed Christians throughout the world are divided. Christians should love one another, but they don't. Hatred, prejudice, and years of misunderstanding and mutual harm divide the Christian church. The interchurch family would like to heal these wounds, but has great difficulty in doing so. This problem is not limited to Catholics. It exists with Protestant couples involved in interchurch marriages as well.

How to solve the dilemma? The couples need much patience. While they long for the day when the church will be one and Christians reconciled, they must live with the present tensions of a divided Christianity. The church can help. *Matrimonia Mixta* was a start. Some suggest that special legislation be established for interchurch couples. They might be treated as a special category with permissions given for their particular needs.

One of the greatest tensions in interchurch marriage is the difficulty in worshiping together. While interchurch couples are now able to go to church together, they cannot normally receive the Eucharist in each other's church. This presents a hardship on special occasions such as weddings, funerals, first communions, confirmations, and the like. While interchurch couples are willing to bear with these difficulties, the churches need soon to provide a more suitable framework for interchurch couples to conduct their lives and to develop spiritually.

August

Creation and Christian Unity

1. The God of All Creation

The World Council of Churches has an important division called *Justice, Peace and the Integrity of Creation.* This division is now working together with the division on Faith and Order on ethical questions.

The Vatican is very much a part of these discussions, because the Catholic Church also believes that justice, peace, and respect for creation are intimately related. Many of the injustices perpetrated in our world center upon the land. Wealth and power have found ways (through war, expropriation and simple theft) to seize the land, leaving the peasant population to live in poverty, or as virtual serfs of the aristocratic and wealthy class.

The multinational corporations have a hand in the perpetuation of this, as do various governments, some of which are either right-wing dictatorial regimes or protected by superpowers who benefit financially from these arrangements. Liberation theology emphasizes that those who read the gospel must also read the signs of the times. They should see the need for reform of many of the existing arrangements.

A Matter of Ethics

Some may consider such ideas political. They are. More importantly they are at the heart of many ethical and social questions that affect people's lives today. One of the ideas that seems difficult for people to grasp is the ethical dimension of the *integrity of creation.* Concern for the earth, sky, water, air, and creation came with the call to the first man and woman to *increase* and *multiply.*

> God blessed them, and God said to them, "Be fruitful
> and multiply, and fill the earth and subdue it; and have
> dominion over the fish of the sea and over the birds of
> the air and over every living thing that moves upon the
> earth." (Gn 1:28)

There are those who interpret this verse as saying humans can
do anything they want with creation. But a more accurate reading
recognizes the *stewardship* that God gives to Adam and Eve over creation. Native peoples have an instinctive sense for the reverence due
to the land and all creatures. Somehow our industrial age and our
technology have lost sight of this imperative.

The God of All Creation

As we head for the beaches and mountains and rivers and
seashores, we should be more aware of the God of all creation and of
the stewardship that is ours over the land. Those who live in the
population centers of our country know the absolute imperative of
conservation and ecology. Without this, our natural resources will
fall victim to irresponsible pollution by industry and uncaring
human extravagance.

We the people are responsible for whatever happens to us and
to creation. The idea that someone else or something else is so over-
powering or powerful as to keep us in perpetual subjugation and
slavery is simply a myth. It takes people to pollute the earth, to allow
oppression, to contribute to the erosion of values in our world and
society. And it takes people to make a difference, to say enough is
enough, and to stay the course of evil.

Edmund Burke said that for evil to triumph it is sufficient for
good men to say and do nothing. He and the Founding Fathers of
our country understood very well that a few good men could stem
the tide of history and reverse the existing order of things.

United in Christ

The ultimate goal of ecumenism is not the comfort of a super church. It is the continuing dialogue and permanent struggle to make the world a better place, the kingdom of God. That struggle will not end until Christ comes again in glory. Meanwhile with a vision of the final triumph of Christ, men and women make that vision a reality each day.

Christian unity is a reality to be recognized. Christ is with his people. He continues to give his Spirit. He continues to conquer the forces of sin and evil. The greed, lust, pride, sensuality and cruelty of the few that keep the many in subjection is the focus of Christ's liberating grace. To work for unity is to work for the triumph of love, grace and salvation.

A Better World

The struggle for the integrity of creation is crucial to the ecumenical movement. A great number of ethical issues are tied together in the struggle for the preservation of natural resources. In many countries the exploitation of forests, rivers, resources and the land is part of the injustice to people, especially to children and the elderly.

The air we breathe, the water we drink, the land we call our own, are all precious to all living things. As we give thanks to God for their abundance, we ask to be made mindful of those who cannot share them as they might or as they should.

2. For the Conversion of the Churches

The *Groupe des Dombes* was founded near Lyons, France in 1937. It began as a group of German and French Protestant ministers who met together to pray for better understanding and peace. Father Remillieux, a Catholic priest, came to hear of the group and began to meet with them for prayer. He told his friend, Abbé Couturier, of his marvelous discovery and Abbé Couturier joined the group.

The Second World War interrupted their meetings, but the meetings resumed after the war. Instead of coming together on the basis of language or country, they met across church lines. Forty members gathered (because that was all the available space in the room where they met at the Trappist Abbey of Les Dombes). The name of the group gradually became identified with the abbey where their sessions were held.

In 1987 the group celebrated its fiftieth anniversary by publishing a book of *memoranda,* which they had written over the years to the churches, both Catholic and Protestant. The title of this book is *Pour la Communion des Eglises* (For the Communion of the Churches). In 1992 they published a second volume entitled *Pour la Conversion des Eglises* (For the Conversion of the Churches).

The *Groupe des Dombes* has had a very great influence on the ecumenical movement in Europe. Some of its members were observers and *periti* at the Second Vatican Council. Though their aim is modest (indeed at the beginning they merely prayed together for unity), they have nevertheless touched the heart of the ecumenical question.

In the 1992 publication, the *Groupe des Dombes* calls for individual conversion and also for conversion at the national and international level of the churches. This is essentially a call to evangelization: what does fidelity to the gospel require of the churches today?

In a series of recommendations the group calls for: a mutual recognition of other churches as one, holy, catholic and apostolic; a moving beyond the *status quo;* and an emulation (trying to outdo one another) in conversion. Specifically they recommend that Protestant churches become more catholic, and that the Catholic Church become a mediator for the other churches, challenging them to be all that Christ calls them to be. Finally the group stresses the need for *real* (not merely symbolic) conversion.

This call to conversion is a profound challenge. It requires that each Christian return to the gospel as the standard for living. It calls for a dissatisfaction with the churches as they are. It calls for *real* conversion, and indeed for a spirit of competition in trying to outdo one another in conversion.

The call to mutual recognition of other churches as one, holy, catholic and apostolic is part of the challenge of Vatican II to its own members to recognize that while the church of Christ *subsists* in the Catholic Church, "some, even very many, of the most significant elements and endowments which together go to build up and give life to the Church itself, can exist outside the visible boundaries of the Catholic Church...." Indeed members of other churches, by virtue of their baptism "are incorporated into Christ; they therefore have a right to be called Christians, and with good reason are accepted as brothers [and sisters] by the children of the Catholic Church" (UR #3).

Can we imagine what such a program would require at the parish level? The *Directory for the Application of Principles and Norms on Ecumenism* (1993) asks Roman Catholics to eliminate divisions within the parish structure. The continuation of bickering between liberals and conservatives on matters that are not *de fide* (of faith) must cease if we are ever to attract other Christians to the unity of the gospel. And other churches, which suffer the same kinds of divisions, must convert to a unity among themselves to prepare for unity among all Christians.

Real conversion means something beyond words. It is conversion in deeds, in truth. Such a massive conversion of all the churches is what is required for Christian unity. Each church wants to think of itself as perfect. But each church must assume its own responsibility for the disunity of Christians.

This is our task as seen by this prayerful group of forty who have met for over fifty years to pray for the unity of Christians. May their prayer, and the prayer of Jesus be heard: *That they may be one...so that the world may believe.*

3. Ecumenism in Western Europe

Thanks to the generosity of my religious community (and some accumulated mileage with an airline), I was able to spend a month one summer in Western Europe. I visited six countries: France (Paris, Lyons, and Taizé), Switzerland (Geneva), Italy (Rome), Austria (Innsbruck), Germany (Munich, Cologne, Düren), and the Netherlands (Nijmegen and Amsterdam).

At each stop I was able to contact ecumenical leaders and visit ecumenical centers: Fr. Guy Lourmande at the Secretariat for Christian Unity in Paris and Fr. Hervé Legrand, O.P. at the Institut Catholique de Paris; Brother John and Brother Hector at Taizé; Fr. René Beaupère, O.P. at the Centre St. Irénée in Lyons; Fr. Max Thurian, Dr. Thomas Best, and Dr. Gunther Gassman in Geneva; the Friars of the Atonement at the Centro Pro Unione (Fr. James F. Puglisi, Fr. Emmanuel Sullivan, Sister Mary Peter Froelicher); Cardinal Edward I. Cassidy and Msgr. John Radano at the Pontifical Institute for Promoting Christian Unity (Vatican), and Fr. A.H.C. Van Eijk at Heemstede in the Netherlands.

These contacts, as well as those with the Blessed Sacrament Fathers and Brothers in these countries, gave me a rather complete picture of what was going on in Western Europe.

What I Learned

One important difference between the ecumenical movement in Europe and in the United States is that Catholics were involved in the movement much earlier in Europe. The St. Willibrord Society in the Netherlands began in 1948. The Groupe des Dombes in Lyons began in 1937. Taizé was established before the Second World War.

Another important factor is that the centers in Europe are staffed by pioneers in the ecumenical movement, like Fr. René Beaupère, who have been contributing significantly to the movement for the past forty or fifty years. These men are extremely qualified. Research centers such as those in Western Europe are few and far between in the United States and other countries. Our centers are only slowly providing the kind of leadership found in Europe.

Different Situation

An important difference between churches in Europe and the United States is the historic difference between Catholics and Protestants there. In Amsterdam I visited one of the Protestant churches that was taken over by the Reformers during the Reformation. At one time it was Catholic, then it became Protestant. People are very conscious of that fact today. These historic differences will need to be overcome by the ecumenical spirit which continues to make progress. However, the pace of progress has slowed, as we are all aware.

Though the church in Western Europe has been weakened considerably by the pervading secularization which has affected the entire world, still there are many hopeful signs. The youth movements in Italy are one such sign. The thousands of youth who flock to Taizé from all over the world, especially during the summer, are an indication that they look to these extraordinary monks to provide inspiration for the future by their dedication to prayer and the unity of Christians.

What We Can Teach

This trip made it clearer to me what the church in the United States can teach. We do not carry as much of the weight of historic divisions as Western Europe. We have a history of cooperation and spiritual sharing. The movements of Europe can help us to develop our own resources, but our gifts can contribute to the worldwide effort to renew the church and Christianity.

The situation in Bosnia clearly points up some of the difficulty in overcoming historic divisions. Eastern Europe has little experience of the spirit of Vatican II and the spiritual ecumenism generated by this great council. The church in the United States can help this ecumenical process.

4. Unity of the Church or of Christians?

Oscar Cullman, renowned scripture scholar and ecumenist, proposes that rather than seek the unity of the church, it might be better to aim at an intermediary goal of a *federation of churches*. Cardinal Ratzinger of Rome's Congregation for the Doctrine of the Faith seems to favor such a proposal. This raises the critical question: what is the goal of the ecumenical movement—unity of the church, or unity of Christians?

Unity of the Church

The clearly-stated goal of the ecumenical movement is the unity of the church. One church, expressed in one faith, one Eucharist and shared decision making, is the vision explicitly stated in the Constitutions of the World Council of Churches. At the General Assembly in Canberra, Australia (1991), the World Council of Churches reached a watershed. Either the Council of Churches would dissolve, or it would make the necessary changes to keep its focus on the unity of the church. Many felt there was far too much politicizing of the General Assembly in pursuit of social and political agendas. The Faith and Order Assembly in Santiago de Compostella in August 1993, hopefully put the World Council back on track. Indeed such a realignment was decided on at Canberra.

For those who think the goal of visible union among the Christian churches cannot be realized, it might be sobering to consider that in 1997 the following proposals for *full communion* were voted on by these dialogues in the United States: Lutheran-Reformed; Episcopal-Lutheran; Consultation on Church Union (COCU) (nine denominations).

There is a proposal for full communion between the Ancient Eastern and Eastern Orthodox Churches (no date). Though there is no concrete proposal for full communion between Rome and the Ancient Eastern and Eastern Orthodox churches, Vatican II declared that these churches are in almost full communion and began to talk of a sister-church relationship between them. The International Theological Commission on Orthodox-Roman Catholic Relations, established in 1982, has as its goal the removal of all obstacles to full communion among all parties.

Unity of Christians

In spite of all the real progress made since Vatican II for real visible unity in Christendom (we should not overlook the many multilateral and bilateral landmark decisions on baptism, Eucharist and ministry which have moved the churches toward full communion), visible unity of all Christian churches is *not* "just around the corner."

Even if the *reintegration* of the church were not to succeed, the unity of Christians would still be a most important goal. And this goal is being reached by leaps and bounds.

One need only remember the suspicion, prejudice and stereotyping of a quarter century ago among Christians to readily assess the progress in this area. Christians do love one another much more today than in the past. Five hundred years of acrimony have given way to profound levels of love, trust and cooperation.

I believe that the prayer of Jesus (Jn 17:21) was much more about the unity of Christians than about the unity of the churches. After over a quarter of a century of work for Christian unity, I am much more sustained by the real success experienced in this regard than by the prospect of the churches being one in our lifetime.

In the final analysis, the Spirit moves us, because of the priestly prayer of Jesus, to both the unity of Christians and the unity of the church. Whatever strategies we advocate in reaching these goals, we must never despair of reaching the unity for which he prayed. *May they be one...so that the world may believe* (Jn 17:21).

Christian-Jewish Relations

1. The High Holy Days

The New Year comes early for the Jewish community. Rosh Hashanah (New Year's Day) and Yom Kippur (the Day of Atonement) are celebrated in the fall; both begin at sunset. These are the High Holy Days of the Jewish Calendar and days of special significance.

Rosh Hashanah begins the New Year with the sounding of the ram's horn (shofar), a trumpet call to rouse the faithful to greater fidelity to the Lord. Yom Kippur is the day Jews ask forgiveness for their sins, and promise to make amends for anything needing correction in their lives. Making things right with God also requires making things right with one's neighbor.

As a member of the local Jewish-Catholic Dialogue, I have attended services at a local synagogue in Albuquerque, New Mexico for these special days. I will long remember the beauty and significance of these High Holy Days. Attending these services is one more sign of the deepening relationship which exists between members of the dialogue, and our desire to share important moments in our spiritual life together.

Signs of Growth and Friendship

In the intervening years the dialogue has done much more than prepare programs promoting better understanding among Christians and Jews. We have become very good friends. We have come to know one another and have grown in our appreciation for each other's faith.

About three years ago the Jewish-Catholic Dialogue began a process of discernment and evaluation that lasted over a year. Long

hours and days were spent determining the nature of the dialogue
and what it hoped to accomplish in the years ahead.

Why Dialogue?

The purpose of dialogue, both ecumenical (Christian) and
interfaith (interreligious), is not always understood. Some see it as a
way of winning converts or scoring for one's own point of view. As a
matter of fact, nothing could be farther from the truth. The purpose
of dialogue is *understanding.*

The Nazi holocaust in Europe and the continuing violence in
the world cry out for dialogue. Religion should be a binding force
among people. Instead it often perpetuates prejudice that leads to
violence. In the concentration camps of the Second World War
many learned to appreciate the faith of their neighbors. They realized that faith sustains people of all religious persuasions.

The Second Vatican Council, especially under the leadership
of Pope John XXIII, helped the church to understand the need for
religious freedom and tolerance. *Nostra Aetate* (on interreligious
relations) and *Dignitatis Humanae* (on religious freedom) are two
documents that emerged from this context.

Since the Second Vatican Council, the church has encouraged
dialogue as a means to better understanding and mutual respect
among Christians and all people of faith. This work continues at the
diocesan level.

Parish Ecumenism

The final goal of dialogue is to change the attitudes of people.
This calls for dialogue at the local level of the parish. Here ecumenism becomes real; people come to know one another in the context of shared faith.

2. Twenty Years of Catholic-Jewish Relations

On October 28, 1965, Pope Paul VI signed the Vatican II document *Nostra Aetate* (In Our Time). With that stroke of the pen he underlined the official attitude of the church today toward other religions. The Jewish faith drew particular emphasis because of the deep roots of Christianity in the Bible and in the Jewish community of which Jesus, Mary and the apostles were a part. Indeed, St. Paul began the impact on the Gentile world through his preaching to Gentile converts to Judaism. Catholics and Jews believe they prepare for the coming of the Messiah and the reign of God. As such they have much in common.

Twenty Years of Growing Unity

Nostra Aetate was not the beginning of Jewish-Catholic collaboration, but Vatican II gave such collaboration a new impetus. It reversed the antisemitism which pervaded the world before and during World War II. The Holocaust dramatized the evil of antisemitism. *Nostra Aetate* called for a new relationship between Christians and Jews:

> Even though the Jewish authorities and those who followed their lead pressed for the death of Christ (cf. John 19:6), neither all Jews indiscriminately at that time, nor Jews today, can be charged with the crimes committed during his passion...the Jews should not be spoken of as rejected or accursed as if this followed

from holy Scripture....Indeed the church reproves every form of persecution against whomsoever it may be directed. Remembering, then, her common heritage with the Jews and moved not by any political consideration, but solely by the religious motivation of Christian charity, she deplores all hatreds, persecutions, displays, and antisemitism leveled at any time or from any source against the Jews. (NA #4)

On June 24, 1985, the Commission of Religious Relations with the Jews issued a document entitled *The Jews and Judaism in Preaching and Catechetics.* The document states:

Religious teaching, catechesis, and preaching should be a preparation not only for objectivity, justice, tolerance but also for understanding and dialogue. Our two traditions are so related that they cannot ignore each other. Mutual knowledge must be encouraged at every level. There is evident in particular a painful ignorance of the history and traditions of Judaism, of which only negative aspects and often caricature seems to form part of the stock ideas of many Christians. (Conclusion #27)

New Attitudes

The church in *Nostra Aetate* and subsequent documents is calling for new attitudes among Catholics. It is calling for mutual respect and collaboration. Ignorance of Judaism is a great loss for Christians because it is ignorance of their roots and much in the tradition of the early church that is reflected in the scriptures and the writings of the Fathers.

If we believe the Jews are the *chosen people* of God with us (as Paul states clearly in Romans 9–11), it is incumbent upon us to work together and to learn from each other. In the light of what our relations ought to be, and what they have been in human history, there is much to lament. But in the light of *Nostra Aetate,* there is much to hope for and celebrate.

3. We Bless You from the House of the Lord

The dedication of the new sanctuary at Congregation Albert in Albuquerque did not receive great attention in the press, but it was an important event for Roman Catholics in the Archdiocese of Santa Fe as, well as for the Jewish community.

I shared the pulpit with distinguished rabbis and with Dr. Wallace Ford of the New Mexico Conference of churches on the day of dedication. It is hard to describe how deeply moved I was on this historic occasion. It reminded me of my visit to the synagogue at Capernaum where Jesus preached, and of the synagogue at Nazareth where he regularly worshiped from his youth to the beginning of his public ministry.

Since Vatican II and *Nostra Aetate,* the Holy See has issued two other important documents: *Guidelines on Religious Relations with the Jews,* and more recently *Notes on the Correct Way to Present Jews and Judaism in Preaching and Catechesis in the Roman Catholic Church.* These documents make it clear that the church is opposed to anti-semitism in any shape or form. More positively the church wishes Roman Catholics to actively foster relations with Jews. This attitude is part of the Vatican Council's theology regarding other religions, and the church's desire to cooperate with all people of faith.

What is special about the Jewish community is that, in the words of *Nostra Aetate,* it continues to hold the promises made by God to his people. St. Paul elaborates this idea in his Letter to the Romans (9–11). Jesus was a Jew, and so he incorporated from his tradition many of the beliefs and practices of our Christian faith. He made it clear he had not come to abolish the "Law and the

Prophets," but to fulfill them. The scriptures (especially the Hebrew scriptures and the psalms), liturgical feasts, worship and prayer, reflect the Jewish origins from which they sprang.

The church is convinced we have much to learn from our religious neighbors, particularly from our Jewish friends. The Jewish-Catholic Dialogue pursues this idea locally, and the Archdiocesan Ecumenical Office gives this interreligious dialogue special importance.

The Jewish-Catholic Dialogue meets monthly. The scriptures, theology, education, family life and topics of social outreach and concern are regularly discussed. The dialogue hopes to develop other groups in the near future at the parish level for discussion and social action.

4. God's Mercy Endures Forever

The guidelines for presenting Jews and Judaism issued by the Vatican in 1985 have been adapted by the Bishops' Commission for Ecumenical Affairs in the United States under the title *God's Mercy Endures Forever*. It is a fitting title for a document that seeks to help American Catholics to understand their Jewish neighbors.

St. Paul in the Letter to the Romans (9–11) probes the mystery of God's plan for his countrymen and comes to the conclusion that God never revokes a promise nor is ever unfaithful to a covenant. Hence God's love for the Jewish people continues in the Christian era.

For Jews and Christians the horror and atrocity of the Holocaust during World War II is difficult to comprehend. How can a kind and merciful God have allowed something so horrendous to happen? John XXIII, in calling the Second Vatican Council, was very intent that a statement on Judaism should be made by the Council. He was convinced the atrocity of the Holocaust should never happen again. Antisemitism in any shape or form could not and should not be justified under the guise of religion. This was the background to *Nostra Aetate,* which incorporated these ideas and established the theological foundation for dialogue and improved relations between Jews and Christians.

As for all conciliar documents, interpretation and implementation is necessary. Since the Second Vatican Council several documents have emerged explaining various aspects of Jewish-Catholic relations. Among the post-conciliar documents perhaps the most important to date is the statement about presenting Jews and Judaism in preaching and teaching. It was issued by both the Pontifical Council for Catholic-Jewish Relations and the Congregation for the Doctrine of the Faith. Dealing with preaching and catechetics, this document touches the very heart of Catholic doctrine.

All of this may seem quite academic. However if one has seen the movie *Schindler's List* and its dramatization of the Holocaust, and followed the development of the Israel-Vatican Accord, and if one is sensitive to growing antisemitism in Eastern Europe and around the world, one realizes that the subject is far from esoteric. This whole area of Jews and Judaism, and their relations to Catholics and Christians, is of the utmost importance.

Holy Week often coincides with the Jewish Passover. History has witnessed many pogroms and outrageous displays of anti-semitism at this most holy Christian time. John XXIII made history by rewriting the liturgical texts for Good Friday. His spirit needs to continue "in our time" (*nostra aetate*). The appropriate understanding of God's mercy with regard to our "elder brothers and sisters in the faith" does not come automatically. Hence the need for continued dialogue and mutual understanding.

5. Torah and Gospel: Love and Law

This topic emerged from a discussion among our Jewish-Catholic Dialogue participants concerning stereotypes about Judaism and Christianity which would tend to see the Hebrew scriptures and the Jewish faith emphasizing law *(torah)* while the Christian scriptures and Christianity stress love *(agape)*. These stereotypes are not true; they are half-truths. Both the Torah (the Books of Moses) and the gospels stress both love and law.

It was the task of invited speakers to point out just how this dual emphasis is exemplified in both the Jewish and the Christian tradition. The topic is challenging and should provide an excellent platform for discussion.

A Lasting Covenant

Underneath the topic for discussion is the hidden idea that somehow Christianity has replaced Judaism, or that only one or the other can be (or is) the true covenant with God. The Second Vatican Council, especially in *Nostra Aetate,* took great pains to point out with St. Paul (Rom 9–11) that God does not abandon his covenants or his promises. The Jews remain the chosen people of God. They are not replaced by Christians, but form with Christians one people that God continues to call to salvation (NA #4).

In the light of the Jewish Holocaust, the Catholic Church has taken a long look at history. The persecution of Jews by Christians is a shameful record which needs to be corrected. *Nostra Aetate* takes as its basic theme the value of all religious traditions, especially those of long standing which have stood the test of time. Among these religions, the faith of Abraham and his descendants has a very special place.

Christianity arose in a Jewish setting. Jesus, his Mother Mary, the apostles, St. Paul and the early followers of Jesus all worshiped in the synagogue and were inspired by the Hebrew scriptures. It was only toward the end of the first century that the break with the Jewish community was definitively made. Eventually Christians felt they were no longer welcome at the synagogue.

Yet the first century of the Christian era was a time of great religious ferment. With the destruction of the Temple at Jerusalem, what began as a rabbinic movement in Israel became a whole new branch of the ancient tradition. The other branch was Christianity, which focused belief in Jesus Christ as the Son of God. Both faiths share common roots and branches in the ancient faith of the people of Abraham recorded in the Hebrew scriptures.

Collaboration and Communication

The purpose of the Jewish-Catholic Dialogue is to help Jews and Christians to come to know one another as people of faith. In this world of materialism and eroding religious values, world leaders see in dialogue between people of faith a hope for the preservation of the basic values of ethics and religion. Family, church and synagogue, home and school need to continue to preserve the values that have created our culture.

Rather than see Jews and Christians in competition, the Second Vatican Council saw them collaborating together for the important issues of peace, justice and the preservation of the environment.

October

Reformation and Christian Unity

1. What We Share in Common

Lutherans and Anglicans seek to preserve as much as possible the tradition of the church which has continued down the ages. They reflect this tradition in liturgical practice and in the emphasis on ordained clergy. The Anglican tradition is given "a special place" in the Vatican II decree on ecumenism (*Unitatis Redintegratio* #13) and Lutherans have enjoyed special attention in the dialogues that have been conducted in the United States and between the Vatican and the Lutheran World Federation.

At the present time an intense study of ordination is under way in the Evangelical Lutheran Church in America, the largest Lutheran Communion in the United States (numbering over eleven million members). This study is particularly focused on the role of bishops in the Lutheran Church.

The Anglican/Roman Catholic Dialogue in the United States recently published an agreed statement on the Eucharist as sacrifice which affirms consensus on this important doctrine.

Women's ordination in the Church of England (the Mother Church of the Anglican Communion) has caused a great deal of controversy in the Church of England and in Rome. This is a new venture for the Church of England, but it was preceded by years of ordaining women in twelve of the Anglican Provinces, including the Episcopal Church in the United States.

The Vatican has reacted strongly to this move because it considers the ordination of women contrary to the ageless tradition of ordaining only men to the priesthood. Anglicans claim a continuity in the historic episcopate and a priesthood identical to what has existed in the church catholic from the beginning. A move to ordain women is therefore an issue of very great importance.

At the present time issues of great significance can be discussed openly and with feeling because the ecumenical movement has moved so far in such a short span of years. From the time of the Reformation, there would have been little reaction to what was done in another church. But thanks to the deep concern for Christian unity, any move by one church is seen to have great repercussions on the others, and on the movement for unity itself.

While the ecumenical movement has lost some interest among people generally, it is of supreme importance to the Catholic Church and Pope John Paul II. New developments are taken very seriously. The dialogue continues, and ways of solving old and new problems are pursued.

2. The Anglican-Lutheran *Concordat*

On January 18, 1991, a proposed *Concordat of Agreement* between the Episcopal Church and the Evangelical Lutheran Church in America was introduced at St. Peter's Lutheran Church in New York City. Presiding Bishop Edmond L. Browning of the Episcopal Church and Bishop Herbert W. Chilstrom of the Evangelical Lutheran Church in America were both present at the announcement and agreed that introduction of the Concordat marks "an important day in the history of our churches."

The Concordat, the text of which was completed in Delray Beach, Florida on January 6, 1991, contains a set of concrete proposals leading to *full communion* between the churches.

The Concordat brings to fruition twenty years of dialogue and initiatives which have brought the churches closer together. As the leaders of the two churches indicated, the Concordat does not fall "in a vacuum." Three successive dialogue teams have studied, written and proposed actions approved by the general assemblies of each church, which have moved the churches to the point where full communion can be contemplated.

One outcome of the Concordat, if adopted by the General Assembly of the Episcopal Church and the Churchwide Assembly of the Evangelical Lutheran Church in America, will be the mutual recognition of ordained ministry across church lines.

Such recognition was conceived and proposed by the World Council of Churches' Faith and Order document finalized at Lima, Peru in 1982 entitled *Baptism, Eucharist and Ministry.* Orthodox and Roman Catholic theologians, as well as a wide spectrum of church bodies, sent representatives to participate in the creation of this convergence document.

The Concordat brings about a number of other important changes in the churches. It bridges one of the most important impasses in the ecumenical movement. Episcopalians require continuity in the *historic episcopate* for the ordination of bishops. Lutherans do not require it and claim that authentic preaching of the gospel and administration of the sacraments are sufficient and the only requirement. In the future bishops from both churches will be present (and required) for all ordination of their bishops.

Bishops in the Lutheran church will be ordained for life, not merely for a term. They will be understood to belong to the college of bishops, not to be merely administrators of the synod (diocese). Priests will be ordained only by bishops in the Lutheran Church (not presently a requirement) as is done in the Episcopal Church.

At this time and only as a single action, the requirements of the Ordinal of 1662 (Episcopal), and subscribing to the Augsburg Confession (Lutheran), will not be required for the mutual recognition of ministry. The appropriate celebration of the Concordat and the mutual recognition of ministries will be worked out by a joint committee of both churches during the coming years.

Canonical, liturgical and theological problems will be ironed out gradually before and after full communion has been achieved. The Concordat will take several years to be approved at various levels. A first vote of the General Convention/Churchwide Assembly was scheduled for 1997. It was approved by the Episcopal General Convention and narrowly missed, by six votes, a required two-thirds vote in the Evangelical Lutheran Church in America. The Lutheran Assembly is committed to approving a revised text of the Concordat in 1999.

Evaluation

For Roman Catholics, as well as for Episcopalians and Lutherans, the progress made in bringing the two churches one important step closer to full communion is to be celebrated. The framers of the Concordat and the leaders of the churches indicate that they have developed a simple, responsible, and practical way of moving the churches toward unity. They admit there is much work to be done before acceptance of the terms of the Concordat is realized. However the degree of unity already achieved in the years since Vatican II is remarkable.

3. Our Standing before God

How do we stand before God? This question was a burning issue for the Reformation. It probably doesn't arouse a lot of interest for modern Catholics. However it remains a vital issue in the dialogue between Lutherans and Roman Catholics.

Martin Luther said that the principle of *justification by faith* (cf. Rom 5:1-3) was so important that the church rose or fell with its stand on this question. This is seen as an exaggeration by Roman Catholics. However it remains very much at the heart of Lutheran belief.

The Issue

The Reformation was a many-faceted reaction to the abuses in the church during the Middle Ages. Discipline was sorely lacking, even at the top of the hierarchy. Seminaries were virtually nonexistent. Superstition colored popular belief and devotion. The need for reform was recognized on all sides. Unfortunately overreaction characterized both the Reformers and the Catholic response. Even bitter wars were fought over religion. Political dimensions were also present. The emperor, the pope, the princes, and the bishops were all involved in what may seem today to have been a high-stakes chess game for power.

It is difficult to sort out praise and blame. Indeed theological issues continue to be debated in the more calm arenas of dialogue rather than on the battlefield. Nevertheless, the Christian Church is terribly divided and the issues remain.

The Lutheran-Roman Catholic Dialogue in the United States made a major contribution to a solution to the controversy in the publication of the seventh volume of its work. The title is *Justification by Faith*. This study has been very well received both by the International Dialogue and by the hierarchies of both churches in the United States.

At the present time the issues involved in this study are being discussed in local conversations. The National Association of Diocesan Ecumenical Officers requested a response from each of the dioceses in the United States, and prepared a report of its findings.

The Council of Trent

In response to the Reformers' question: how do we stand before God? the Council of Trent answered that we are justified, provided we have faith in the saving grace of our Lord Jesus Christ. The Reformers answered with Martin Luther that we are both just and sinners *(simul justus et peccator)*. Today we see that both answers leave something to be desired. The liturgy invites us at each Eucharist to confess our sinfulness before God. Thus we recognize our sinfulness even though we are about to celebrate and receive the Eucharist. Luther's response that God "overlooks our sins" and looks rather at the justice of Jesus Christ, also runs into problems with the clear indication of the scripture that justification is real, and the Christian stands before God in the state of grace.

Unity in Reconciled Diversity

How can we reconcile these different points of view? The Lutheran-Roman Catholic Dialogue suggests that these views are complementary. Lutherans look at the grace of God and stress its primacy; Catholics look at human freedom and assert its importance. The way we can break through our disunity is to work for unity in reconciled diversity. This means that we try to reconcile our differences, while realizing that our positions will never be entirely the same. The points of view are too different for ultimate conformity. However there can be an acceptance of our differences for the sake of genuine unity. The Lutheran and Roman Catholic position today—that we are *justified by grace received in faith*—is an example of such reconciliation.

Lutherans and Roman Catholics have much in common. A strong affirmation of Christian faith, high moral standards, careful celebration of the liturgy, are characteristics of both churches. Among the several dialogues presently under way in the church, the Lutheran dialogue holds an important place, along with the Anglican dialogue, in the West. At the level of diocese and parish, there is much we can share together.

4. Unity in Diversity

One topic that is frequently discussed in Lutheran-Roman Catholic dialogues is unity in diversity, or reconciled diversity. In a local discussion of the topic some time ago the theme was: *Unity in Diversity: The Next Steps.*

In discussing the theme, the presenters feel progress toward unity among the churches of the "catholic" tradition will require, in addition to prayer and patience, a great deal of openness to diversity in the search for unity.

The church catholic has, in its long tradition, been able to tolerate much diversity. It was able to inculturate itself in cultures as diverse as those of Asia Minor and North Africa, Rome and Greece, England and France. Differences of liturgy, canon law, theology, symbol and imagery abound not only in New Testament times, but throughout the history of the church.

Diversity in the New Testament

A careful reading of the New Testament, especially the writings of Paul and the Acts of the Apostles, reveals that there were profound differences among the early Christians. The church at Jerusalem and the church at Antioch were Jewish and Gentile, respectively. How to incorporate the gospel in a Gentile culture was very difficult for the apostles and early disciples of Jesus. It was mostly thanks to St. Paul that the task was made at all possible. Peter himself wavered on this point, though he knew from a revelation (Acts 10:1-47) that the gospel should not be restricted to the Jews.

At the Council of Jerusalem (Acts 15:6ff) it was decided that only the essentials would be imposed on the Gentile converts. In nonessentials complete freedom was to be allowed.

This pattern can be seen in the early church. St. Cyprian (d. A.D. 258) in particular was its champion (see his letters to Pope Stephen). In the first centuries of Christendom, even in the West, diverse rites and customs developed and were encouraged by the church of Rome.

Catholicity and Diversity

Many Catholics today identify catholicity with uniformity. As a matter of fact the term means the opposite. To be catholic is to be able to embrace the whole world (*kath olos*). In other words, it requires being open enough to tolerate the inculturation of the one faith (unity) in many different cultures, times and settings. This is the glory of the church catholic, and the story of its journey through the ages.

Unfortunately in the sixteenth century, because of the attacks of the Reformers on Catholic Church teaching, the church of Rome responded with a counter-reformation that stressed uniformity and a defensive and polemical attitude.

The story is well known. The church, after the Council of Trent, made diversity difficult. Indeed, the church in the last five centuries is characterized more by its pursuit of uniformity than a promotion of diversity.

Vatican II seeks to reverse this emphasis. The process requires more than mere tolerance. It requires a search for truth and a response to the prayer of Jesus *that all may be one...so that the world may believe.*

The Unity We Seek

The unity we seek is not purchased at the expense of legitimate diversity. Quoting the Acts of the Apostles, Vatican II emphasizes that in the church renewed and visibly reunited, only what is essential will be required. Nonessentials will be left to the judgment and discretion of other Christian churches.

While preserving unity in essentials, let all members of the church, according to the office entrusted to each, preserve a proper freedom in the various forms of spiritual life and discipline, in the variety of liturgical rites, and even in the theological elaborations of revealed truths. In all things let charity be exercised. If the faithful are true to this course of action, they will be giving ever richer expression to the authentic catholicity of the church, and, at the same time, to her apostolicity. (*Unitatis Redintegratio* #4)

November

The Communion
of Saints

1. The Eucharist and the Communion of Saints

November reminds us of the Communion of Saints and the final resurrection which awaits us all. We move into the heart of the fall season and death is all around us. But we know that as nature moves from harvest time to winter, it also moves into the hope of spring's return. New life and resurrection will grow beneath the snow and burst forth into the joy of spring.

Similarly our spiritual life deepens in hope as we reflect upon our mortality and the Communion of Saints. This article of our faith is not always in the forefront of our thinking, but it should always be in the depths of our soul. We are in communion with Jesus Christ, Mary, and the saints in a real and deep communion. This communion which began in baptism is nourished by the Eucharist. It is at the heart of what it means to be Christian and of our hope for Christian unity.

Saint Paul called the Christians of his time "saints" (from *sanctus,* holy) and it is an appropriate name not only for those who die in grace, but also for all who live in God's favor. On November first we celebrate the feast of All Saints and remember all those who have died in Christ. These saints number not only the canonized, those officially recognized by the church as being in heaven, but also those not so recognized. Many of these we have known and loved. This *multitude of witnesses* we hope to join one day. We are in communion with all of the saints who share the holiness of Jesus Christ.

Indeed we are in communion with all who are in Christ, living or dead. Catholic teaching tells us we can even assist by our prayers those who have died but are not yet in heaven. In *The Dream of Gerontius,* Cardinal John Henry Newman helps us to understand that these souls are detained from their final reward by a suffering not measured by earthly time. Any delay in being embraced by God's love and glory is an intense suffering for those who long to be with Christ in the full communion of the blessed.

There is another communion that is equally important, the communion of all living Christians. This communion includes, in the teaching of Vatican II, not only those Christians who are in full communion by virtue of their baptism and faith in Jesus Christ within the Catholic Church, but *all* Christians in every Christian church that joins its members together with Christ by faith and baptism.

We are in almost full communion with all Christians of the Orthodox Churches. We are in real though imperfect communion with all Christians of the Reformation Churches because they too are joined to us by faith and baptism.

The ecumenical movement is the work of the Holy Spirit, we are told in Vatican II's *Unitatis Redintegratio,* moving all Christians toward full communion. This communion will be perfect in heaven, even though at this time it may be imperfect on earth.

Realized Eschatology

The ecumenical movement seeks what theologians call *realized eschatology,* that is, the realization of God's kingdom in time. The kingdom of God is something to be realized fully in heaven. However it is the paradigm, the model, for what Christians must build in the earthly city. When we pray *thy kingdom come* we are praying for the final realization of God's will for us. We are also praying that we may be empowered to realize that "will" in our time and in our space.

The Eucharist

The Eucharist is the sign of God's kingdom, the sacrament of the Body of Christ which we receive and which we become. The Communion of Saints means that we are united by every Eucharist to Jesus, our Lord, and through him with every member of his body, living and dead, in glory and in transit to heaven. We are joined at one common table, the Lord's table, and will one day be joined together in the banquet of heaven.

Realized eschatology means realizing in our time the kingdom of God that is yet to come. Eternity will be the celebration of the coming of the kingdom. The Eucharist is the celebration of its anticipation and sacramental proclamation.

2. The Full Communion of Saints

Each year we celebrate the feast of All Saints. Our secularized society makes much ado about the Eve of All Saints (Halloween), and it is a lot of fun for children. But they need to know about the *All Hallows* of which Halloween is the eve.

Stephen Carter in *The Culture of Disbelief* points out that at the heart of the overall problem in our culture is the *trivializing* of religion. Religion is treated as a joke or not taken seriously. Though freedom of conscience is given lip service, religion itself is not promoted.

On a visit to Philadelphia for the annual meeting of the North American Academy of Ecumenists, I visited some of the historic churches around Independence Mall. I also saw the headquarters of the American Philosophical Society of which Benjamin Franklin and Thomas Jefferson were prominent members. These Founding Fathers did not want to trivialize religion nor relegate it to a private hobby. On the contrary, they were very explicit about the need for religion in America. Unless religion is honored and religious groups exercise their influence on government, no democracy is possible. According to Alexander de Toqueville, religion in America guarantees the success of the "American Experiment."

The Communion of Saints

Reflecting on the beginning of our country and the end of time can be helpful. We focus on our goals and the means to attain them. Ultimately we are destined to spend eternity with God. We will either rejoice in his friendship or bemoan our eternal damnation. The choice is ours. We are saved by grace and faith in God. We are condemned by rejecting God's love.

The Vatican Council teaches that God wills the salvation of all. The church taught this truth from the beginning: For God so loved the world that he gave his only Son, so that everyone who believes in him may not perish but may have eternal life (Jn 3:16). The ecumenical movement believes that God wants to save everyone and uses the means of salvation that are shared by all Christians and all men and women of faith.

> It follows that the separated Churches and communities as such, though we believe they suffer from the defects already mentioned, have been by no means deprived of significance and importance in the mystery of salvation. For the Spirit of Christ has not refrained from using them as means of salvation which derive their efficacy from the very fullness of grace and truth entrusted to the Catholic Church. (UR #3)

Salvation will bring us all into the *communion of saints*. We believe that all those who love God are in communion with him. Christians are in communion with God by faith, hope, love and baptism into the Body of Jesus Christ. This communion in God and in Christ will reach its summit in heaven. There we shall be glorified with all the saints in the joy and transformation of the resurrection. Our task is to praise God with all the angels and saints—even now. Our final fulfillment is to join the angels and saints in joyful praise of God for all eternity.

We Shall Be Changed

St. Paul indicates that at the resurrection we shall be like the Risen Lord. We shall be changed. Our corruptible body will put on incorruption:

> Listen, I will tell you a mystery! We will not all die, but we will all be changed, in a moment, in the twinkling of an eye, at the last trumpet. For the trumpet will sound,

and the dead will be raised imperishable, and we will be changed. For this perishable body must put on imperishability, and this mortal body must put on immortality. When this perishable body puts on imperishability, and this mortal body puts on immortality, then the saying that is written will be fulfilled: "Death has been swallowed up in victory." (1 Cor 15:51-54)

Ecumenical Implications

Since the beginning of the 1990s various churches have proposed moving toward mutual recognition of ministries and full communion. Between 1996 and the year 2000 several churches will decide to be in full communion with each other. The Lutheran and Reformed Churches worldwide were to have decided by 1997 for a status of full communion. Several churches of the Consultation on Church Union (nine denominations which grew out of the Reformation in Europe and Methodism in the United States) responded affirmatively to a proposal for full communion, and the remainder are expected to do the same in the coming years. The Lutheran and Episcopal churches in the United States similarly are working for full communion through a Concordat of Agreement.

This should be the subject of much prayer, reflection and dialogue at this time. It will require decisions for reconciliation among the churches. We should remember the communion of saints because we are a part of it and are destined to share it completely in God's kingdom.

3. I Call You Friends

Anyone familiar with the Middle East realizes that hospitality is a cultural trademark. Eating together is a sign of that hospitality. Bible scholars are quick to point out that Jesus frequently ate and drank with others. In fact the Scribes and Pharisees reproached him for eating and drinking with sinners.

Meals are not only an occasion for hospitality to travelers, they are also opportunities for deepening friendships. It should be no surprise, then, that at the Last Supper Jesus said: "I will no longer call you servants but friends" (Jn 15:13).

The small band of followers of Jesus, especially the Twelve, had every reason to believe they were the friends of Jesus. But why this special insistence on it? Jesus gives the reason, in part at least, by pointing out he has revealed the Father to them and all they needed to know about him.

Reflecting on these words of Jesus, I see a further meaning in the statement about friendship. The Eucharist continues for the church what Jesus celebrated with his apostles. Jesus gave the church a banquet of friendship. Paul (in 1 Corinthians) and John (in his first letter) describe the Eucharist and the church (1 Cor 10:16-17; 1 Jn 1:3-4) as a fellowship with Christ, in the Spirit, and with all Christians. God binds Christians together in the life of the Father shared with Christ. The Eucharist develops this life given at baptism, hence the Eucharist is called the Bread of Life (cf. Jn 6:48ff).

This fellowship among Christians is not limited to members of one church. Ecumenists see in the prayer of Jesus "...that all may be one" (Jn 17:20) a challenge to work for unity among all Christians.

Thus is established the theological foundation for ecumenism, namely, unity in Christ and fellowship among all Christians.

Sometimes clergy wonder how they can become more ecumenical. The first step is friendliness. Joining a ministerial alliance or study group, or simply inviting a local minister for coffee is a good start. The laity will find the same prescription effective. Parish committees on ecumenism hosting ecumenical prayer, dialogue or Bible study are important parts of parish life in the church today.

"I call you friends" is an important eucharistic statement of Jesus. It is one that will carry us far in the task of Christian unity.

December

Advent, Christmas, and Christian Unity

1. In Him Is Our Hope

Jesus Christ is our hope. In him dwell the divine and the human. Our hope of transcending our human limitations, of living to our full human potential and of touching the divine come from Jesus Christ. God dwells in mystery. And some of that mystery was revealed in the coming of Jesus Christ. "And the Word was made flesh and dwelt among us; and we have seen his glory" (Jn 1:14).

> Our hope is in Christ. He is the light of the world, that enlightens every man and woman. The faithful should remember that they promote union among Christians better, that indeed they live it better, when they try to live holier lives according to the Gospel. For the closer their union with the Father, the Word, and the Spirit, the more deeply and easily will they be able to grow in mutual brotherly love. (UR #7)

And so our focus must be on Christ, our hope. *En Lui è la nostra pace* (In him is our peace—Dante Alleghieri). We are at peace as we walk the gospel path because we know that our growth in Christ is growth in truth. The truth will set us free and is the way to peace.

The Eucharist—Christ's Mass

Christ, Prince of Peace, was born on Christmas. We celebrate his "Mass," his birth, death and resurrection in the Eucharist. And in this celebration we already possess the goal of unity: the oneness of faith, Eucharist, and church.

Throughout the world all Christian Churches and peoples celebrate the Word made flesh. We are one in the profession of the firm belief that God took human form so that we might become his children. Transcending human limitations is visible in Jesus Christ. In his service of compassion, forgiveness, love and unity we see how human beings become divine. Through the Bread of Life we are strengthened to continue to walk in hope. Our hope for the world and for the unity of the human family is in Jesus Christ.

Searching for God

Karl Rahner describes faith in God as the search of restless hearts for the ultimate meaning and the underlying reality of all that is. This ultimate goal of our quest and restless hearts lives in mystery. In Jesus Christ the hidden mystery has been revealed. The world that walks in darkness has seen a great light. Jesus, the light of the world, shines in our darkness and enlightens our hearts.

We begin to understand the meaning of life—our life—as we understand the meaning of Jesus' life. We can only know the Father if he is revealed to us by the Son. We can only call Jesus Lord in the Spirit. And we can only love God as we discover the Father, Son and Spirit in our hearts.

The hope for the human race is not in technology. It is not in politics or economics. It is in Jesus Christ, Savior of the world. Born in a stable, laid in a manger, bereft of everything except the essentials of human life, Jesus teaches us what it means to be human and what it means to be a child of God.

Conclusion

In 1999 we celebrate the last Christmas of this millennium. A thousand years of unity were followed by a millennium of separation and division among Christians. Pope John Paul II prays that we make every effort in the coming years to prepare a millennium of unity and communion among all those who believe in Jesus Christ as Son of God and Savior of the world.

We pray that our celebration of Christmas may open our minds and hearts to the Spirit of the Risen Lord so that we may share more deeply in his life, his hope, and his prayer for the unity of all Christians.

2. Prince of Peace

Pray for the peace of Jerusalem. (Ps 122:6)

A dramatic chapter in the struggle for peace in Israel includes the brutal slaying of Yitzhak Rabin, president of Israel. Like Jesus who lived and died for peace, Rabin devoted his life to bringing peace between nations; he is a martyr for the cause of peace. Jesus was born to bring "peace on earth and good will to all" (Lk 2:14). He is the Prince of Peace.

Peace is an elusive reality. It is more than the cessation of war or a dangerous balance of power *(Gaudium et Spes)*. It must constantly be reborn and recreated. Peace requires forgiveness and reconciliation. The peace that Jesus came to bring is fundamental peace between God and humankind. In Hebrew the term *shalom* means complete harmony between persons and within the individual. To be at peace means that "all is well with my soul" and I walk in peace with my God. As we celebrate the feast of Christmas, we pray for inner peace, and that the peace announced by the angels may reign in the world.

The Jewish community celebrates the feast of lights at this time of year. Hanukah is remembered in each Jewish home by the lighting of a nine-branched candle or *menorah*. Like our progressive lighting of the four candles on the Advent wreath, the *menorah* basks the Jewish home in an ever- growing aura of light.

The light of Christ is the symbol for his grace, his life and his Spirit that flood our souls and radiate in our homes. Prince of Peace, Jesus came to bring the reign of God, the kingdom of peace, to all who walk in God's ways.

The difficult struggle for peace at the world level reflects the inner struggle for peace and serenity in each one of us. We must pray for peace because it is God's gift. We cannot achieve genuine and lasting peace without the healing gift of God's amazing grace.

Justice and peace cannot be separated. If we want peace, we must work for justice. The World Council of Churches adds that peace and justice must also include the integrity of creation. The peaceful balance of nature is part of the search for the integrity of human relationships. Often the exploitation of the land is part of the unjust exploitation of people. Peace on earth requires respect for all God's creation.

Peace entails harmony with God, serenity within oneself, and concord with others. It begins with inner serenity within the individual. We cannot be at peace with others unless we are at peace with ourselves.

Peace requires forgiveness and reconciliation. Concord with others results from this generous spirit of forgiveness and desire to heal old wounds. Such reconciliation brings peace and harmony. But inner personal peace is God's gift and results from the harmony that exists between human beings and their God. Amos described this relationship as "walking humbly with God": He has told you, O mortal, what is good; and what does the Lord require of you but to do justice, and to love kindness, and to walk humbly with your God? (Mi 6:8).

The peace of nations grows out of this relationship with oneself and God. If we seek God's will and his kingdom, we will work for his justice. Very often a climate of war is created by one nation reaching into the territorial integrity of another. War is caused by economic inequality, unjust trade relations, the greed of a stronger nation over a weaker one, or the envy of a lesser nation for the power and wealth of a stronger one.

Our country is one of the mightiest in history. But it is in danger of being very selfish. Rather than embrace a peaceful policy of live and let live, we are embarking on a protectionist policy that is built on pride, selfishness, greed and unjust pursuit of our own interests. Such a policy has led to war in the past. It can do so again.

As we prepare for the Third Millennium, we pray for the peace of Jerusalem, the City of God. We pray that peace may come to us from the Prince of Peace, and that the inner harmony of our lives may radiate in the global peace the world desperately needs.

3. Christmas and Christian Unity

"Peace on earth to those on whom his favor rests" (Lk 2:14). The greeting of the angels on the first Christmas night gave glory to God and prayed that peace might come to men and women through the Prince of Peace, Jesus Christ, born in Bethlehem.

The peace of the angels' song was for the whole world. And that peace rests in the hearts of people more than in the calm produced by armies. The Prince of Peace came "to gather into one the dispersed children of God" (Jn 11:52). This task of reconciliation was not limited to the Jewish population. It extends to everyone.

The Unity We Seek

The feast of Christmas is a celebration of Christian unity. All Christians believe in the same Lord and Savior, Jesus Christ. We worship the same God, keep the same commandments, share the same hope of salvation and eternal glory. We are members of the Body of Christ which is the church—even though a church divided.

What is the unity we seek? It is not the unity of a federation of churches or a megachurch embracing everyone in a faith which is the common denominator of all. Rather, it is a deepening and growing communion (*koinonia*) of all Christians in the peace (*shalom*) which Jesus Christ came to bring to the world.

This unity is a *recognition* of our common faith and our shared baptism in Jesus Christ. Christian unity is not something to be created. It is something to be recognized as already existing, thanks to the grace of Jesus Christ who gives his Spirit and his life to all who believe in him.

The result of Christian unity is a growth in respect, cooperation and united efforts to bring God's kingdom to visible realization in our world. In Jesus Christ the will of God the Father to save all human kind appeared (Ti 2:11). In the unity of Christians this will to save is made visible in our time and in our world.

A More Complex Goal

The goal of Christian unity seemed very simple and easily achievable in the days after Vatican II. That goal is more complex and more difficult today. The difficulty comes from a greater awareness that more than "one big church" is required. Christian unity means a deeper communion of all Christians in Christ and with one another. Vatican II talked about the necessary reform of Catholic Christians. A similar transformation is required of other Christians as well.

Theological dialogue continues to reveal the many issues that remain unresolved since the Reformation. The resolution of these issues must be achieved, if unity is to be possible. Like current social problems, they will not go away by blaming one side or the other. We are all part of the problem; we must all be part of the solution.

Can we build a wider circle to embrace all those Christians who are outside the circle of our church or personal belief? That is the critical question for Christians today.

Mary and the Church

Mary is the Mother of Jesus and the model of the church. She gave human life to Jesus so that he might give eternal life to all of us. Mary loves us all because Jesus saved us all. She wants the unity of all her children because unity in Christ is the will of God the Father. That is why Jesus came. That is why he prayed: "Father, may they be one as we are one...so that the world may believe..." (Jn 17:21).

4. The Mystery of Christ

It is a beautiful sunny day and three inches of snow covers the ground, the first snowfall of this season. A very picturesque scene spreads out before me. Just a couple of days ago I noticed some beautiful geese swimming in the lake outside my door. Now it is partially frozen from the night's cold and the geese are gone. Though Christmas is weeks away, it is easy for someone raised in New England to write about Christmas in this brisk, wintry setting.

My research at the Institute for Ecumenical and Cultural Research some years ago was a project about the Eucharist as sacrifice. What it taught me about Christmas is that when we celebrate the Eucharist we offer the same sacrifice that Jesus presents forever to our Father in heaven. It is obviously the sacrifice of the cross, the high point of self-offering in Jesus' life. And Jesus offers us and our sharing in his life.

The Eucharist is the whole *mystery* of Christ: his incarnation, his childhood at Nazareth, his public life, his preaching, his miracles, his suffering and death, his resurrection and glorification. As many prefaces of the mass indicate, we meditate and give thanks for one or the other facet of this great mystery in each Eucharist. Pope Leo I in his magnificent homilies for Christmas describes how we *celebrate* the mystery of Christ; how we share in it through the liturgy.

Christmas, then, is our sharing in the self-giving of Jesus. When he entered our world and our history he said: "In the beginning of the book it is written of me...behold I come to do your will, O God" (Heb 10:5-7).

Christmas is a memorial and sharing in the self-offering of Jesus. He came "for us and for our salvation." More than a recalling of the birth of Jesus in history, Christmas is a sharing, through the Eucharist, in the salvation Jesus brings to each of us on this day.

Feast of Faith

The Ecumenical Institute is located in the atmosphere of prayer, quiet reflection and study of St. John's University and the abbey of Benedictine monks who founded it and teach there. I have had time to reflect a great deal on the place of faith in our lives. In the humdrum of our busy lives we either take faith for granted, or often do not develop its full potential for meaning in our lives.

Christmas is an opportunity for us to focus our faith once more on the most important event of human history: God's gift of his Son for our salvation. "He will be called Jesus, because he will save his people from their sins" (Mt 1:21).

We believe that Jesus is the Son of God. We believe that he is the icon of God's love for us. He is our friend and brother who shares his life with us, as we accept his invitation to sit down at table with him in the Eucharist.

As we gather family and friends around our dinner table for Christmas joy, Jesus gathers us around his table to share the deepest meaning of this day. "Unto us is born a savior, who is Christ the Lord" (Lk 2:11).

5. Born to Us a Savior

> For the grace of God has appeared, bringing salvation to all, training us to renounce impiety and worldly passions, and in the present age to live lives that are self-controlled, upright, and godly, while we wait for the blessed hope and the manifestation of the glory of our great God and Savior, Jesus Christ. He it is who gave himself for us that he might redeem us from all iniquity and purify for himself a people of his own who are zealous for good deeds. (Ti 2:11 – 14)

Each year we meditate on the meaning of Christmas. The incarnation of God, the Word becoming flesh for our salvation. The reason for the life of Jesus Christ is "because he will save his people from their sins" (Mt 1:21). We don't often reflect on salvation. But it is very important to our faith. We believe that humanity is in a sorry mess because of sin. Without redemption/salvation, people are sinful and capable of the worst of crimes. "But for the grace of God there go I" is a humble acknowledgment of the rooted sinfulness which exists in each of us.

Salvation is the opposite of condemnation. If we are saved, we are not lost. The Anglican-Roman Catholic International Commission's statement on *Salvation and the Church* puts it this way:

> The will of God, Father, Son and Holy Spirit, is to reconcile to himself all that he has created and sustains, to set free the creation from its bondage to decay, and to draw all humanity into communion with himself. Though we, his creatures, turn away from him through sin, God continues

to call us and opens up for us the way to find him anew. To bring us to union with himself, the Father sent into the world Jesus Christ, his only Son, in whom all things were created. He is the image of the invisible God; he took flesh so that we in turn might share the divine nature and so reflect the glory of God. Through Christ's life, death and resurrection, the mystery of God's love is revealed, we are saved from the powers of evil, sin and death, and we receive a share in the life of God. (SIC #1)

While our meditation on the Christmas scene centers on the mother and child of Bethlehem and the pastoral scene of the stable, with the child lying in a manger, our ultimate focus should be on the purpose of this birth, "for us and for our salvation" (Nicene Creed).

Born to Us a Savior

Our gift-giving at Christmas should be a reflection of God's great gift to us, a Savior. We share the joy that is ours and God's generosity by the generosity we extend to others, especially to the poor. Christmas is a time for giving alms to our favorite charity. It is a time to remember the gift of friends and the gift of the love we share. In turn we show our love and gratitude by the gifts we give.

God's greatest gift is his Son who became our Savior by taking on a human nature like our own. It was in his human nature that he saved us, by suffering and dying for us and by rising from the grave. Thus he saved us from sin and death and gives us faith and hope in our own resurrection.

Eucharist

The Eucharist is the presence of our Savior who continues to save us from sin and death by his Paschal Mystery. The Word became flesh. He became our Bread of Life so that we might become children of God, living lives that are self-controlled, upright and godly. Thus we await the coming in glory of our Savior Jesus Christ who saves us and purifies us, his people, who are zealous for good deeds.

6. In Bethlehem of Judea

Jesus was born in Bethlehem of Judea during the reign of Augustus Caesar, while Quirinus was governor of Syria (Lk 2:1-2). Christians and Jews, unlike many of the religions of the past, believe in a God who is part of human history. Indeed the God of all creation intervened in critical ways throughout the history of humankind. He continues to do so today.

Jesus was part of time, of history, and of a culture. He was born in Palestine, in Judea. He was therefore a Jew. Mary and Joseph were Jews. The apostles (Peter and Paul, James and John) and all of the disciples of Jesus were Jews. Indeed the early Christians were all Jews until Barnabas went to Antioch and Paul went with him throughout the Mediterranean to spread the good news of salvation in Jesus Christ.

Jesus loved his race and his countrymen. He said he had come to call the lost sheep of Israel. He did not preach to the Gentiles. He left that to his followers. In the light of this early history, one wonders what happened to bring about the kind of antisemitism that arose in the second century and developed throughout the centuries. The *shoah* (holocaust) during World War II was the most horrible example of this antisemitism.

Even the Fathers of the Church, like John Chrysostom, were not exempt from antisemitism. Some gospel passages seem to be tainted with it. No wonder then that it continues to our day. Father Edward H. Flannery writes that it is difficult for Christians to realize the antisemitism they have breathed in with their culture. Eradicating this racism is an important task for Christians today. Vatican II calls for such renewal and the gospel itself challenges Christians to it.

Jews and Christians Today

Both Christians and Jews believe that God intervenes in human history. The Jews believe that God revealed himself to Abraham, the founder of the Hebrew race, and to Moses, their great lawgiver. Christians believe that God intervened in human history by sending Jesus Christ of Nazareth, the Son of God, to redeem mankind. This is the deepest reason for celebrating Christmas.

The separation of the church and the synagogue occurred in the second century. It was unfortunate. Had the church really understood what St. Paul wrote to the Romans (ch. 9–11), it would never have encouraged the kind of animosity and hatred which grew in the centuries that followed. Paul writes that God does not retract his covenants or go back on his promises.

> I ask, then, has God rejected his people? By no means! I myself am an Israelite, a descendant of Abraham, a member of the tribe of Benjamin. God has not rejected his people whom he foreknew...for the gifts and the calling of God are irrevocable. (Rom 11:1-2, 29-30)

As we join the millions of Christians of many church traditions in celebrating the birth of Christ, we are conscious that we owe a great debt of gratitude to our Jewish brothers and sisters. The Jewish community received God's covenants and nurtured faith in the one God, creator of the universe. Into that faith community Jesus was born and from it the church began.

As our Jewish brothers and sisters celebrate Hanukah and the winter holiday, we celebrate the birth of Christ and Christmas. We pray for the fulfillment of the angels' song: "Glory to God in the highest and on earth peace to those on whom his favor rests" (Lk 2:14).

7. The Grace of God Has Appeared

> For the grace of God has appeared, saving all and train-
> ing us to reject godless ways and worldly desires and to
> live temperately, justly, and devoutly in this age, as we
> await the blessed hope, the appearance of Jesus Christ,
> who gave himself for us to cleanse for himself a people as
> his own, eager to do what is good. (Ti 2:11–14)

Christians throughout the world will join in celebration on
December 25th, remembering the birth of our Lord Jesus Christ. The
unity of the church is most visible on this day when Christians from
every tradition celebrate the great mystery of the Word become flesh.

We often focus our attention on the babe in the manger and
the nostalgic memories of days of yore. Paul's letter to Titus suggests
we focus equally on the present and the future. The grace of God
has appeared; we have seen God's love in the life, death and resurrection of Jesus his Son. This appearance and grace which give us
salvation from our sinfulness is a call "to reject godless ways and
worldly desires." We are called to live justly, temperately and
devoutly. We hope and await the appearance of our Lord Jesus
Christ in glory.

God and Man

The awesome mystery of God, the creator of the universe,
coming to earth simply defies understanding. Our imaginations are
powerless to describe what this means. But we know the babe in the
manger became the Savior of the world on the cross, and the Lord of

heaven in the resurrection from the dead. This child is the Savior, the one who brought God's gracious favor to all of us. We are God's children because we are brothers and sisters of Jesus Christ by the power of God's grace.

Salvation has been explained in many ways by different churches of Christendom. In recent years through dialogue divided voices have found a new harmony in one expression of one faith in Jesus Christ, Savior of the world, who saves us by God's grace which we accept in faith.

But we are saved *for* something. We are saved *for* good works. As God's people, we are challenged to build his kingdom. As his children we are called to resemble the Father. We are commanded to love one another as children of one human family. Seen in ecumenical perspective, this call is a challenge to work together for the good of all. We do not build God's kingdom in isolation, but together we work for the peace, justice and love which characterize that kingdom.

We await the coming of "our blessed hope," the Lord Jesus who comes in glory with salvation for his people. The communion of saints in glory will achieve the kind of unity we have prayed for and worked for on earth. And this communion has already begun. Because God has graced us with his Spirit and life in his Son, we have already begun to taste the eternal banquet. The Bread of Life is given to us in the Eucharist so that we may deepen our hope for a full share in the glory of God. The gift of the Son and the Spirit are the first fruits of the full gift of the Father's glory.

We rejoice therefore and give fond wishes of Merry Christmas to each other. The mass we celebrate is a thanksgiving to God for the gift of his Son, our Savior. It is also the cause for our jubilation. "Joy to the world and peace to all of good will."

8. Christmas and Christian Unity

What has revealed the love of God among us is that the only-begotten Son of God has been sent by the Father into the world, so that, being made man, he might, by his redemption of the entire human race, give new life to it and unify it. Before offering himself up as a spotless victim upon the altar of the cross, He prayed to his Father for those who believe: "that all may be one, as you, Father, are in me, and I in you; I pray that they may be one in us, that the world may believe that you sent me" (Jn 17:21). In his Church he instituted the wonderful sacrament of the Eucharist by which the unity of the Church is both signified and brought about. He gave his followers a new commandment to love one another, and promised the Spirit, their Advocate, who, as Lord and life-giver, should remain with them forever. (Decree on Ecumenism #2)

Christmas is a time when we experience the unity of Christians almost tangibly. Our communion with Christ deepens as we celebrate his coming in history and in grace. It is the latter that is at the very heart of Christmas—too often forgotten in the hustle and bustle of our consumer society.

We recognize Jesus as Lord, sent for the redemption of the entire world, and "to unite the divided family of God" (Jn 11:52). We are one in faith with all those who make the same confession. Those who are baptized in Christ form one Body. Thus, all Christians form that core of unity which God wishes for all of humanity.

At this holiday season we frequently hear statements about peace, good will, and brotherhood. Rightly so. Those who believe in God as Father of all realize, if they are Christians, that God's plan seeks to bring all creation into one in Christ. This central theme from the writings of St. Paul should make our celebration of Christmas a jubilee for unity. In Christ we are saved by being freed from sin so that our divisions may cease and we may be united as the family of God.

There is a tendency among us (and it isn't easy to overcome) to think of Christmas in denominational terms. We think of Catholics celebrating the feast of Christmas, as though it were an exclusively Catholic feast. While we *do* celebrate Christmas in a unique tradition, we are not alone in celebrating the feast. Orthodox and Protestant Christians also celebrate Christmas. In many instances the very same customs and ceremonies characterize their celebration. This common celebration of Christmas should help us to remember to acknowledge our unity throughout the year. *We are one in Spirit; we are one in the Lord.*

9. The Year of Jesus Christ, Son of God

The three years of immediate preparation for the third millennium began with a year dedicated to reflection on Jesus Christ, the Son of God. The year A.D. 2000 will celebrate the 2000th birthday of Jesus Christ, the Son of God, before we enter the third millennium of Christianity.

Lord of History

Jesus Christ is the Lord of history. He has this title because he is the Son of God. He has it because the coming of Jesus was a remarkable moment in the history of humanity and of salvation. John's Gospel states: "No one has ever seen God. The only Son, God, who is at the Father's side, has revealed him" (Jn 1:18).The incarnation of the Son of God is filled with mystery. And it is precisely this mystery that we are asked to contemplate as we move forward to another landmark in history, the coming of the third millennium.

Jesus of Nazareth is a unique individual. That is why all human history in our society is marked by the approximate date of his birth. He is the Anointed of God (Messiah, Christ). Whether we believe that Jesus is the Christ or not, his arrival on the scene has profoundly marked all of human history.

The Word of God Proclaimed

The apostolic proclamation *(kerygma)* is clear. Jesus is the Christ and the Son of God. The sign that marks this reality is his resurrection and ascension to God in glory. Peter first made this proclamation on Pentecost morning when the Jews inquired about the descent of the Holy Spirit on the disciples of Jesus: "Therefore let the whole house of Israel know for certain that God has made him both Lord and Messiah, this Jesus whom you crucified" (Acts 2:36). Stephen made a similar proclamation before the Sanhedrin (Acts 7:56). Paul is clear and articulate in his proclamation of Jesus Christ as Son of God (Acts 13:38 and Rom 1:3-7). Similarly John's Gospel (and the Synoptics as well) was written so that we might believe that Jesus is the Christ, the Son of God (Jn 20:31).

Life in his Name

Jesus Christ, the Son of God, entered human history so that we might have life eternal. The life which comes from the Father and is fully in his Son by the incarnation, is ours through faith, hope and love. Those who believe in Jesus as the Son of God begin to share his divine life. We are given the abiding gift of the Holy Spirit who pours out God's love into our souls and enables us to call God "Father" (*Abba*) and Jesus Christ, "Lord" (*Kurios*) (Gal 4:6; 1 Cor 12:3).

Faith is a divine gift and a human choice. The divine initiative requires the human response. And thus the divine touches the human, the incarnation is reenacted over and again in human history as the Body of Christ is formed, with Christ as the head and us as his members.

Eucharist

The Eucharist needs to be part of our reflections throughout this time of preparation for the millennium. The year A.D. 2000 has been designated as the Year of the Eucharist. The Holy Father has called for an International Eucharistic Congress in Rome during that year. The Eucharist is the abiding presence of Jesus Christ, the Son of God. His sacrifice is available to us in the liturgy and his presence is "for us" in the eucharistic sacrament.

The purpose of all creation is the worship of God. All things and all ages proclaim his glory. We are swept up in this hymn to God and his marvelous works as we prepare a very special birthday, the 2000th of Christian history. And having celebrated it, we will begin to live in the third millennium.